Integrated IT Ass.ig......

Integrated IT Assignments

Barry Mc Gettigan

Gill & Macmillan

Gill & Macmillan Ltd
Goldenbridge
Dublin 8
with associated companies throughout the world
www.gillmacmillan.ie

© Barry Mc Gettigan 2000
0 7171 2989 6

Print origination by Graham Thew Design

The paper used in this book is made from the wood pulp of managed forests. For every tree felled, at least one tree is planted, thereby renewing natural resources.

A catalogue record is available for this book from the British Library.

For James

Contents

Part 2 Concepts

Acknowledgments

I would like to thank all those who have helped me with this book. Thanks to Adam Brophy and all the staff in Gill & Macmillan for their helpful advice. Thanks to my very understanding wife Dymphna without whose help this book could not have come to fruition.

How to Use This Book

Each project in this book is made up of three components: a spreadsheet, database and word processing assignment. These components are linked together to form a complete project reflecting real-life examples. So, it may be necessary in some projects to complete one component before you can move on to the next one, which may require data from the previous component. You can access the Web site for this book, which contains files for most of the database components so that you can focus on learning rather than entering data. You can download the files from the following Web site:

http://www.gillmacmillan.ie/integratedsolutions

The scenario for each project is described at the beginning of each project. The estimated time for completion and a difficulty rating are also given. The ratings are in the range from one to five: one being fairly easy and straight-forward and five being more challenging. The projects are grouped according to their rating value. A list of the knowledge skills that you need to complete each project is also given. The page numbers where each skill is explained are listed in the Skills table. The projects become progressively more challenging and rely on previous skills, and so you build a complete framework of knowledge as you work through the projects.

This book is intended for students who already have some computer experience. You can progress at your own pace (within the estimated time), or you can proceed to the next project if you have time to spare. Some students may be able to work ahead on their own, because the skills required are listed at the start of each project.

You can also use the projects to build up a substantial folder of work demonstrating your IT skills. The work can then be easily assessed; for example, number of projects completed and standard of work.

Part 1
Projects

Project 1

The project is set in a video store. You are required to create a simple spreadsheet showing annual sales. You will then create a database, which the video store owner can use to enter new videos and check out films for rent. You then use a word processor to create a letter.

Time   The estimated time for this project is two and one-half hours.

Rating   This project has a difficulty rating of one.

Skills   You need the following skills to successfully complete the project:

Software Package	Tasks to Complete	Explanations (see pages)
Spreadsheet	Create, insert/copy formula, chart	139, 141
Database	Create, data entry form, insert rows, query	131, 132, 134
Word processing	Formatting	125

Project 1
DATABASE

Magik Video requires a database, which will be used daily to track stock movement. Create the database structure using the following field names, widths and datatypes:

FIELD NAME	WIDTH	DATATYPE
CUSTOMER	20	Text
VIDEO	20	Text
DATE OUT	8	Date
DATE DUE	8	Date
PRICE	5	Currency
ARREARS	5	Currency

Create the following data entry form to facilitate data entry:

MAGIK VIDEO	
Customer_____	Date Due _____
Video _____	Price _____
Date Out _____	Arrears _____

After making the data entry form, insert the ten records below. This database tracks whether a video is overdue.

CUSTOMER	VIDEO	DATE OUT	DATE DUE	PRICE	ARREARS
J WILLIAMS	Alien	12/2	14/2	€2.50	0
B CARLING	Waterworld	11/3	13/3	€2.50	0
K KEANE	Mad Max	12/3	14/3	€2.50	0
M MURDOCK	Grease	10/3	12/3	€2.50	0
R PETERS	Titanic	10/1	12/1	€2.00	0
L MURPHY	First Strike	12/3	13/3	€2.00	0
J FERRY	Airforce 1	12/3	13/3	€1.50	0
J JORDAN	Red Storm	11/3	11/3	€1.50	0
M MACARI	Goldeneye	9/3	10/3	€2.00	€2.50
S WESTON	Titanic	8/3	9/3	€2.50	€4.50

1. If today's date is 12 March, check whether any videos are overdue (Hint: check the DATE DUE field for dates before 12 March.)
2. The arrears column checks for any arrears that haven't yet been paid. Search for customers who have to pay arrears and print this list.
3. Two customers have just rented two videos. Insert the following two records to update the database:

C FERRY	Scream	12/3	13/3	€2.00	0
S FIRTH	Titanic	12/3	13/3	€2.50	0

4. Check for any customers who have rented Titanic and print a list of these customers.
5. Print the complete database.
6. Save the database as VIDEO.

Project 1
SPREADSHEET

1. Create the spreadsheet below which will determine the annual sales in the video store.
2. Determine and insert the formula to calculate the total for the Total row. Copy this formula across columns B, C and D.
3. Insert a formula in column F to determine the total for each row for the year. Copy this formula to the remaining rows.
4. Create a chart showing the *total* for each quarter.
5. Print a copy of the spreadsheet and a copy of the chart. (Hint: if your printer does not support colour, use patterns in black and white.)
6. Save the spreadsheet as VIDEO.

	A	B	C	D	E
1	Sales for year 2000				
2					
3		Jan-Mar	Apr-Jun	Jul-Sep	Oct-Dec
4	Video	€10,345	€8,956	€8,034	€12,223
5	Food	€5,660	€5,100	€4,899	€11,200
6	Merchandise	€1,200	€1,100	€900	€890
7					
8	Total				
9					

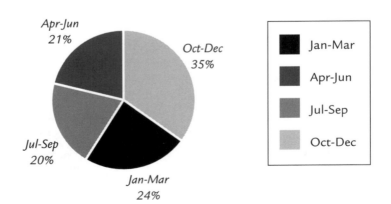

Apr-Jun 21%   Oct-Dec 35%   Jul-Sep 20%   Jan-Mar 24%

Jan-Mar
Apr-Jun
Jul-Sep
Oct-Dec

In this section, you create the following letter, and enhance it using bold, italics and underline:

MAGIK VIDEO LTD
Donbander Road
Eastpark

Your Name
Your Address
Date

Dear Name,

We note from our records that you have the following videos outstanding:

Titanic   12 April to date
Goldeneye   13 April to date

The arrears that you owe amount to €12.56. We would appreciate it if you would return the videos immediately and pay the amount owed.
If the videos are not returned by 17 April, we will be reluctantly forced to cancel your membership.

Sincerely,

J Martin
Manager

1. Create the letter as shown above.
2. Put the words *Titanic* and *Goldeneye* in bold.
3. Put the word *immediately* in italics.
4. Put the word *cancel* in bold and underline it.
5. Print one copy and save the file as VIDEO.

'If the automobile had followed the same development cycle as the computer, a Rolls Royce would today cost $100, get one million miles to the gallon, and explode once a year killing everyone inside.'
Robert X Cringley

Project 2

In this project you will prepare a document for a plumber, create a database showing customers, last callout, fee etc. You will also create a simple spreadsheet to determine the cost of a job.

Time The estimated time for this project is two hours.

Rating This project has a difficulty rating of one.

Skills You will need the following skills to successfully complete the project:

Software Package	Tasks to Complete	Explanations (see pages)
Spreadsheet	Create, insert/copy formula	139, 141
Database	Create, data entry form, query, add records	131, 132, 134
Word processing	Formatting, non-proportional fonts	123, 125

Project 2

DATABASE

ABC1 Plumbing Services require a database to be created, which will be used to track customers. The database will use a data entry form (below) to facilitate data entry. Create the database using the following information:

FIELD NAME	WIDTH	DATATYPE
CUSTOMER	15	Text
ADDRESS	15	Text
TELEPHONE	7	Numeric
DATE	8	Date
WORK	15	Text
COST	4	Currency
PAID	1	Yes/No

Create the following data entry form:

```
+------------------------------------------------------------+
|                    ABC1 PLUMBING LTD                       |
|                                                            |
|   Customer  _____      Address  _____          |
|   Telephone _____      Date     _____          |
|   Work      _____      Cost     _____          |
|   Paid      _____                                    |
+------------------------------------------------------------+
```

After making the data entry form, insert the following ten records:

CUSTOMER	ADDRESS	DATE	WORK	COST	PAID
G Wilson	12 East St	12/2	Drain	€120	Y
R Roberts	23 Main St	23/3	Drain	€120	Y
K Yates	12 Main St	24/3	Burst pipe	€60	Y
P Jones	2 Old Rd	12/2	Heating	€200	N
O Brougham	4 New Rd	30/3	Burst pipe	€40	N
N Conlon	45 Will St	17/2	Heating	€250	Y
M O Neill	28 Gray St	27/3	Drain	€150	Y
D Broderick	1 Park St	25/1	Drain	€130	N
E Robinson	56 West St	23/1	Burst pipe	€40	Y
S Firth	23 East St	12/3	Heating	€200	Y

This database will track customers to see whether they've paid their bills. It will also be useful for tracking the most common type of repair. The TELEPHONE NUMBER field is not shown, add your own to the database. Do the following:

1. Search for work carried out that has not been paid for.
2. Search for work carried out on drains.
3. Search for work carried out on burst pipes.
4. Search for work carried out in Main St.
5. Insert the following two records:

R Worth	53 West St	21/1	Burst pipe	€40	Y
M Sheridan	31 East St	14/3	Heating	€200	N

6. Perform the search in question one again for unpaid work.
7. Print the results of this search.
8. P Jones has just sent in a cheque for the work carried out. Make the necessary adjustments to the database.
9. Save the database as PLUMBER, and print one copy of the complete database.

Create the following spreadsheet. It is an example of a template; that is, you can use it repeatedly simply by changing the values in the cells:

	A	B	C	D
1	ABC1 PLUMBING			
2				
3		Call-Out	€40	
4		Labour	€15.00	
5		Hours Worked	1.5	
6		Replacement Pipe	€23.00	
7		Subtotal		
8		VAT @ 21%		
9		Total		

1. There is a standard call-out charge of €40.00, which is the data in C3.
2. Labour is charged at a rate of €15.00 per hour (C4).
3. The total number of hours worked was 1 hour 30 minutes (C5).
4. The replacement pipe cost €23.00 (C6).
5. To calculate the subtotal you must calculate the labour cost (multiply C4 by C5), and add this cost to the call-out charge and the cost of the replacement pipe.
6. You must add VAT at 21% to the Subtotal. Multiply the value in C7 by 21% and insert the answer in C8.
7. Finally, add the subtotal to the VAT to find the total cost of the work.
8. Enhance the spreadsheet as you see fit. For example, use bold for column B and italics for column C.
9. As an example of how this spreadsheet can be used as a template, try the following:
   • Change the hours worked to 2.3.
   • Change the words in B6 to *Valves and Washers.*
   • Change the data in C6 to €20.89.
   The spreadsheet recalculates the result based on the new values.
10. Save this file as PLUMBER and print one copy.

The plumber has drafted the following letter to a customer detailing the work done and the cost. The company name is typed at the top of each letter. He uses a non-proportional font to enhance the letter as follows:

ABC1 PLUMBING SERVICES
2 Castle Street, Oldcastle

Ms M Kennedy
Main Street
Oldcastle

Date

Dear Ms Kennedy,

The following details the *emergency* work carried out on your premises on 12 February and the associated cost:

```
Call-out charge        €40.00
Replacement pipe       €23.00
Labour                 €15.00
Total                  €78.00
```

Thank you for choosing *ABC1 PLUMBING SERVICES* for carrying out this work.

Sincerely,

---

1. Create the letter shown above.
2. Change the company name and address to a non-proportional font.
3. Change the work costs to a non-proportional font.
4. Enhance the letter as shown using bold, italics and underline.
5. Sign the letter with your own name and print one copy.

'Whom computers would destroy, they must first drive mad.'

Anon

Project 3

This project looks at how the IT needs of a taxi firm are integrated. You will create a flyer for the taxi firm, a database of their customers and a spreadsheet showing the account of one customer.

Time   The estimated time for this project is two hours.

Rating   This project has a difficulty rating of one.

Skills   You will need the following skills to successfully complete the project:

Software Package	Tasks to Complete	Explanations (see pages)
Spreadsheet	Create, insert/copy formula	139, 141
Database	Create, data entry form, query, add/delete records	131, 132, 134
Word processing	Margins, copy, formatting	125, 122, 125

Project 3
DATABASE

JO-MAXI TAXIS use a database to track customers, to find out how often customers use their services and where they are going to etc. The database uses a data entry form (below) to make data entry easy. Create the database using the following information:

FIELD NAME	WIDTH	DATATYPE
CUSTOMER	15	Text
ADDRESS	15	Text
TELEPHONE	6	Numeric
DATE	8	Date
JOURNEY	10	Text
FARE	4	Currency

```
┌─────────────────────────────────────────────────────────┐
│                    JO-MAXI TAXIS                          │
│   Customer  _____     Address  _____          │
│   Telephone _____     Date     _____          │
│   Journey   _____     Fare     _____          │
└─────────────────────────────────────────────────────────┘
```

After making the data entry form, insert the following ten records:

CUSTOMER	ADDRESS	TEL	DATE	JOURNEY	FARE
T Nelson	12 East St	334567	13/4	Airport	€12
T Ferry	23 Main St	445636	12/4	Train	€8
G Norton	12 Main St	853552	15/5	North	€7
E Maguire	2 Old Rd	556244	12/3	North	€7
H Thornton	4 New Rd	356722	26/4	Train	€8
E Robinson	45 Will St	767432	9/4	South	€4
A Sweeney	28 Gray St	423676	7/4	Train	€8
A Grier	1 Park St	664178	12/5	West	€6
P Rooney	56 West St	235842	13/4	Airport	€12
M Mc Cafferty	23 East St	574794	17/3	East	€6

This database is used to track customers with accounts in the taxi firm.
1. Search for all fares to the airport and print one copy.
2. Search for fares costing less than €7.00.
3. Remove the record for G Norton, because she has moved to another town.
4. Add the following two records:

Your Name	6 West St	236742	13/4	Airport	€12
J Mc Cafferty	3 East St	573474	7/3	East	€6

5. Repeat the search in question one again for fares to the airport.
6. A watch was found on 13 April in one of the taxis. Search for journeys on 13 April to see whom it might belong to.
7. Search for journeys going to the train station.
8. Save the database as TAXI and print one copy of the complete database.

The following spreadsheet calculates the account of a customer for one month:

	A	B	C	D
1	JO-MAXI TAXIS			
2	Account for	E Robinson 01/2000		
3				
4	Date	Fare	Vat @ 21%	
5	5/01	€10.50		
6	7/01	€12.46		
7	9/01	€13.48		
8	15/01	€10.50		
9	16/01	€12.34		
10	18/01	€10.90		
11	20/01	€15.56		
12	25/01	€13.59		
13	Admin	€20.00		
14	Subtotal			
15	Total			

1. Create the spreadsheet. Insert a formula to calculate the VAT in C5 (multiply B5 by 21%).
2. Copy this formula to the remaining cells down as far as cell C13.
3. Insert a function to calculate the subtotal in cell B14 and copy this function to C14.
4. Insert a function to calculate the total in C15. (Hint: add the subtotals of B14 and C14.)
5. Enhance the spreadsheet as you see fit.
6. Save the file as TAXI and print one copy.

A taxicab company has created a flyer and an advertisement to enhance its profile. The advertisement is as follows:

JO-MAXI TAXIS LTD.

FREEPHONE 0800 JOMAXI

For FAST results, freephone this number and book your taxi.
NO CALLOUT CHARGE!
OUR PROMISE — If we don't collect you within 30 minutes, your fare is free!
SPECIAL AIRPORT DEALS from €8.00 (between 10 a.m. and 4 p.m.).

1. Create the advertisement above.
2. Enhance the advertisement as you see fit (e.g. use centre, underline etc).
3. Save the file as TAXI. Then create the following flyer:

JO-MAXI TAXIS LTD.

FREEPHONE 0800 JOMAXI

HAPPY BIRTHDAY!

JO-MAXI taxis have just celebrated over ten years in business. We want to thank you for the continued support that you have shown over the years. As a small gesture of thanks for your business, present this coupon to get 20% off your next fare.

Our motto is 'We're here to get you there'. Our goal is to do this as quickly as possible, without breaking the bank. If we don't keep our promises, you get a free fare and that's a guarantee!

1. Set a left margin of 1.5 inches and a right margin of 1 inch.
2. Enhance the flyer as you see fit.
3. Copy the advertisement and paste it after the last line in the flyer.
4. Delete the last line of the advertisement.
5. Save the file as FLYER and print one copy.

'Never trust a computer you can't throw out a window.'

Steve Wozniak

Project 4

In this project, you will see how a clothing factory uses and combines different IT applications in the workplace. You will use the word processor to place orders for products. You use the database to keep a record of each employee, absences etc. You create a spreadsheet to calculate the salary for an employee.

Time   The estimated time for this project is two hours.

Rating   This project has a difficulty rating of one.

Skills   You need the following skills to successfully complete the project:

Software Package	Tasks to Complete	Explanations (see pages)
Spreadsheet	Create, insert/copy formula	139, 141
Database	Create, data entry form, query, sort	131, 132, 134
Word processing	Margins, sanserif fonts	125, 124

Project 4
DATABASE

Morecambe Design, a clothing factory, uses a database to keep a record of each employee. The database uses the fields listed below. Create a data entry form similar to the following:

FIELD NAME	WIDTH	DATATYPE
EMPLOYEE	15	Text
ADDRESS	15	Text
TELEPHONE	6	Numeric
SECTION	1	Text
ABSENCES	1	Numeric
WORKDAYS	2	Numeric

```
                    MORECAMBE DESIGN
    Employee  _____   Address   _____
    Telephone _____   Section   _____
    Absences  _____   Workdays  _____
```

After making the data entry form, insert the following ten records:

EMPLOYEE	ADDRESS	TEL	SECTION	ABSENCES	WORKDAYS
G Doherty	12 East St	334567	A	0	20
T Ferry	23 Main St	445636	B	2	18
M Sheridan	12 Main St	853552	D	0	20
J Friel	2 Old Rd	556244	E	0	20
H P Friel	4 New Rd	356722	A	4	16
E Robinson	45 Will St	767432	B	0	20
M O Hara	28 Gray St	423676	B	2	18
C Robinson	1 Park St	664178	A	0	20
C Vaughan	56 West St	235842	C	1	19
M Mc Cafferty	23 East St	574794	D	0	20

This database is used to keep track of employees' workdays on a monthly basis. Do the following:

1. Sort the database by section.
2. Search for employees who were not absent in the past month.
3. Print a list of the employees who were absent in the last month.
4. Insert two new records as follows:

J Ferry	6 West St	227842	D	1	19
Your Name	3 East St	574794	D	0	20

5. Search for employees in Section D and print the results of this query.
6. T Ferry has not shown up for work today. Search the database to find her telephone number.
7. Save the database as CLOTH and print one copy of the completed database.

The following spreadsheet calculates the pay for an employee for one month. (It is simplified for the purposes of this book.)

	A	B	C	D
1	MORECAMBE	DESIGN		
2	Employee	T Nelson		
3		Hourly Rate	€7.00	
4		Overtime	€11.00	
5				
6		Hours Worked	40	
7		Overtime	4	
8		Bonus	€40	
9		Gross		
10		Tax @ 24%		
11		Net		

1. In cell D6, insert a formula to calculate the pay due based on the number of hours worked. (Hint: multiply the hourly rate by the number of hours.)
2. In cell D7, insert a formula to calculate the overtime due.
3. In cell C9, insert a formula to calculate the gross pay (including the bonus).
4. Insert a formula in C10 to calculate the tax payable.
5. Finally in cell C11, calculate the net pay.
6. Save the file as CLOTH.
7. Enhance the spreadsheet as you see fit.
8. Use the spreadsheet to calculate the wages for A Sweeney using the following information:
   • Hourly rate is €8.00
   • Overtime rate is €13.00
   • Number of hours worked is 45
   • Overtime worked is 5
   • Bonus is €50
9. Print one copy of the spreadsheet.

A clothing factory wants to place an order for supplies. The following information is given:

- Cloth serial number
- Colour
- Number of reams required

Morecambe Design
Unit 54
Western Industrial Estate

Cloth Direct
12 Main Street
Newcastle

Date

Dear Mr Johnson,
Please forward the following as soon as possible:

Serial No	Colour	Number
11223	Midnight Blue	12
22334	Cerise Pink	8
22455	Lavender	9
66533	Terracotta	15
33244	Sea Mist	6
43332	Baby Pink	9
22355	Autumn Harvest	7
55392	Pacific Blue	6
99322	African Red	2

Sincerely,

---

1. Set the left margin at 1.5 inches and the right margin at 1 inch.
2. Choose a sanserif font for the cloth colours.
3. Enhance the letter as you see fit.
4. Insert the following order between serial numbers 33244 and 43332:
   - 12255
   - Saffron
   - 5
5. Sign the letter with your own name, and print one copy.
6. Save the file as CLOTH.

'Hardware: the parts of a computer that can be kicked.'

Jeff Pesis

Project 5

This project looks at how IT applications can work together in an activity centre. You use the word processor to create a document showing the various activities on offer. The database shows the dates of booking, the number, the cost etc. A spreadsheet shows the cost for each group.

Time   The estimated time for this project is two hours.

Rating   This project has a difficulty rating of one.

Skills   You need the following skills to successfully complete the project:

Software Package	Tasks to Complete	Explanations (see pages)
Spreadsheet	Create, insert/copy formula	139, 141
Database	Create, data entry form, queries using AND, OR	131, 132, 134, 135
Word processing	Margins, headers, serif font, enhance	125, 124

Project 5
DATABASE

The Westpool Activity Centre uses a database to schedule the timetable of activities according to date, group size, cost and contact person in charge of each group. The database has the following structure:

FIELD NAME	WIDTH	DATATYPE
DATE	8	Date
GROUP SIZE	2	Numeric
ACTIVITIES	25	Text
COST	3	Currency
CONTACT	15	Text
TEL	6	Numeric

WESTPOOL ACTIVITY CENTRE

Date   _____   Group Size_____

Activities   _____   Cost   _____

Contact   _____   Tel   _____

After making the data entry form, insert the following ten records:

DATE	GROUP SIZE	ACTIVITIES	COST	CONTACT	TEL
24/5	10	Windsurfing, Kayaking	€250	J Maguire	334567
25/5	12	Orienteering	€300	H Simpson	445636
23/5	10	Windsurfing	€250	C Kent	853552
24/5	8	Kayaking	€200	B Ferry	556244
24/5	6	Archery, Kayaking	€150	A Firth	356722
27/5	24	Canoeing, Orienteering	€600	M O Loony	767432
26/5	12	Windsurfing	€300	M R Sweeney	423676
27/5	13	Archery, Canoeing	€325	J Mc Cafferty	664178
28/5	15	Canoeing, Orienteering	€375	J Mc Philips	235842
28/5	8	Kayaking, Archery	€200	S Clarke	574794

1. The kayaking course has been cancelled. List all groups who want to do kayaking.
2. Events on 24 May are scheduled to begin one hour later than advertised. List all the events on 24 May.
3. Insert two new records:

29/5	15	Canoeing, Orienteering	€375	Your Name	232342
30/5	8	Kayaking, Archery	€200	K Egan	564784

4. Search for groups that have archery as an activity.
5. Search for groups that have canoeing as an activity.
6. Print the complete database, and save the file as ACTIVITY.

Project 5

SPREADSHEET

This spreadsheet calculates the cost of a group booking, which depends on the season, whether accommodation is included or whether a discount is applicable etc.

	A	B	C	D
1	WESTPOOL	Activity Centre		
2				
3			High	Low
4		Cost/Person	€20	€15
5		Accommodation	€25	€20
6		Discount (>20)	5%	10%
7				
8	Number in Group	15		
9		Cost		
10		Accommodation		
11		Discount		
12		Subtotal		
13		Vat @ 21%		
14		Total		

1. Create the spreadsheet above.
2. Insert a formula in cell C9 to determine the cost for a group of fifteen in high season. Insert a similar formula in cell D9.
3. Insert a formula in cells C10 and D10 to determine the accommodation costs.
4. Discounts apply only to groups of twenty or more, so do not enter the formula at this stage.
5. Calculate the Subtotal and copy it to D12.
6. Calculate the VAT applicable in C13, and copy it to D13.
7. Calculate the total in C14, and copy it to D14.
8. Find out what the cost is for a group of twenty-three people in the low season. (Hint: remember to include the discount.)
9. Save the file as ACTIVITY and print one copy.

The activity centre has been asked to provide information on activities and costs for a group of fifteen people requiring accommodation during the high season. Create the following reply using a serif font:

SAILING AND ACTIVITY CENTRE
Westpool Marina

Phone — 01 1342656 Fax — 01 1342657

Re: Quotation

Dear James,

Thank you for your enquiry regarding the activity centre. We offer the following activities. Please note that the times cannot be changed:

Kayaking	9.00 – 12.00
Canoeing	9.00 – 12.00
Windsurfing	13.00 – 17.30
Orienteering	13.00 – 17.30
Archery	Any Time

Costs per person range from €15 in low season to €20 in high season. Accommodation costs range from €20 per person in low season to €25 in high season. Discounts apply for groups of fifteen or more.
For further information, please don't hesitate to contact me.

Sincerely,

1. Set a left margin of 1.25 inches and a right margin of 1.5 inches.
2. Create a header and insert the name, phone and fax number of the centre.
3. Change the word *fifteen* to *twenty* in the last line of the third paragraph.
4. Enhance the letter as appropriate and sign it using your own name.
5. Save the file as ACTIVITY and print one copy.

'Who's General Failure and why is he reading my disk?'

Anon

Project 6

In this project, which is set in a web design company, you will see how Spyder Web Design uses IT applications to carry out everyday tasks. You will create a database of potential clients that the company can target for work. You will use a word processor to send a letter to existing clients. Finally you will create a spreadsheet to calculate the cost of designing and maintaining a web site for the client.

Time   The estimated time for this project is one and one-half hours.

Rating   This project has a difficulty rating of one.

Skills

Software Package	Tasks to Complete	Explanations (see pages)
Spreadsheet	Create, insert/copy formula, charts	139, 141
Database	Create, data entry form, queries using AND	131, 132, 134
Word processing	Margins, headers	125

Project 6

DATABASE

Spyder Web Design, a company specialising in the Internet business, has created a database to target potential customers. This database (called WEB) is on the Web site. It consists of the following fields:

- COMPANY — Name of the company
- SIZE — Number of employees
- TURNOVER — Turnover per year
- AREA — Products that the company makes
- CONTACT — Name of person to contact
- TEL — Telephone number

FIELD	WIDTH	DATATYPE
COMPANY	15	Text
SIZE	3	Numeric
TURNOVER	6	Currency
AREA	12	Text
CONTACT	12	Text
TEL	6	Numeric

Retrieve the file WEB from the Web site. It contains the following information:

COMPANY	SIZE	TURNOVER	AREA	CONTACT	TEL
Print1	52	€155,000	Print	T Nelson	334567
Micromos	50	€180,000	Textile	T Ferry	445636
RemPrint	58	€200,000	Print	G Norton	853552
LartLo	300	€2,000,000	Textile	E Maguire	556244
Kemdot	20	€90,000	Print	H Thornton	356722
SafeNuc	300	€2,500,000	Nuclear	H Simpson	224245
Electro	200	€130,000	Electrical	J Spark	438297
KemiKal	57	€334,000	Chemical	M Currie	982232
Kosmic	332	€442,000	Cosmetic	D Druff	429432
NucSafe	455	€3,500,000	Nuclear	M Burns	448322

1. The company RemPrint has ceased trading. Remove this record from the database.
2. Search for companies with more than fifty employees.
3. Search for companies with a turnover of more than €150,000 per year.
4. Add the following two records to the database:

Kemm	332	€442,000	Cosmetic	P Connors	554432
Q-Print	45	€307,000	Print	A Glynn	498322

5. By analysing its previous sales, Spyder Web Design wants to target companies with a turnover of €150,000 or more per year and who have at least fifty employees. Create a query that fulfils both these criteria. Save this query as TARGET.
6. Spyder Web Design knows that sales in the print area are sluggish. It wants to remove these records from the TARGET query. Remove all records in the area listed as print.
7. Print the TARGET query.
8. Save the database as WEB.

Project 6
SPREADSHEET

Spyder Web Design has designed the following spreadsheet to provide an accurate quote for clients who want to use the services of the company to create a web site.

	A	B	C	D
1	Spyder Web Design			
2			Cost	
3		Design (per page)	€70.00	
4		No. of pages		
5		Total cost of design		
6		Domain registration	€140.00	
7		Site Mirror	€200.00	
8		Uploading	€150.00	
9		Maintenance (per quarter)	€150.00	
10				
11		Subtotal		
12		Vat @ 21%		
13		Total		

1. Create the spreadsheet and calculate the total cost for a site containing five pages.
2. A client wants a quote for design only. How much does it cost for two pages?
3. Another client wants to receive a quote for the following:

   • Designing a web site with ten pages
   • Registering the company name as a domain name
   • Uploading the site
   • Setting up a site mirror

   (Note: the client does not want to avail of maintenance.)
   How much will this service cost?
4. Create a chart showing how the cost is broken down.
5. Save the file as WEB and print one copy.

Spyder Web Design wants to inform its customers about the various products it offers. It has drafted the following letter for circulation to all its clients:

Spyder Web Design
HTML House
Parkway Street

Date

Dear Customer,

The following is the revised product listing for this year including the new (reduced) prices for designing your corporate web pages:

Design   €60 per page
Uploading   €50 per 2MB
Maintenance   €200 per year
Domain registration   €70
Mirror Server   €200
Three e-mail addresses   free

We hope to continue to serve your needs in the future. Should you have any queries, please do not hesitate to contact Caroline Ferry at 01 6242424, or e-mail her at cferry@spyderdesign.com.

Sincerely,

1. Set the left margin at 1.25 inches and the right margin at 1.5 inches.
2. Put the company name and address in a header.
3. Use the word processor to automatically insert the date.
4. Choose a non-proportional, sanserif font for the prices quote.
5. Enhance the letter as you see fit.
6. Sign it using your own name.
7. Save the file as WEB and print one copy.

'If a train station is where the train stops, what's a workstation?'

Anon

Project 7

This project is set in a pottery factory. You are going to create a letter, which lists the various items manufactured by the factory. You also create a database that lists the various artists who supply pottery to the factory. Finally, you create a spreadsheet that calculates how much each artist is owed.

Time   The estimated time for this project is two hours.

Rating   This project has a difficulty rating of two.

Skills   You need the following skills to successfully complete the project:

Software Package	Tasks to Complete	Explanations (see pages)
Spreadsheet	Formula, copy	139, 141
Database	Data entry form, queries using AND, OR, sort	132, 134, 135, 132
Word processing	Superscripts, bulleted list, margins, headers, footers	127, 128, 125

Project 7
DATABASE

The Rustic Pottery Co. uses a database to track when an artist is due commission. The database is set up as follows:

• Artist — Name of the artist
• Area — Area the artist works in
• Date — Date the artist handed in work
• Paid — Whether the artist was paid
• Fee — Fee the artist is due

FIELD NAME	WIDTH	DATATYPE
ARTIST	15	Text
AREA	10	Text
DATE	8	Date
PAID	1	Yes/No
FEE	3	Currency

Retrieve the database file RUSTIC from the Web site. It contains the following information:

ARTIST	AREA	DATE	PAID	FEE
J Gradowski	Paint	12/5	Y	€120
D Brennan	Glazing	13/4	N	€135
O Brougham	Paint	16/6	Y	€230
P Jones	Design	13/4	N	€128
A Sweeney	Design	18/6	Y	€109
S Kerr	Paint	12/3	Y	€240
A Greir	Glazing	25/4	Y	€190
J Marin	Paint	28/4	Y	€175
P Smith	Design	12/5	Y	€180
V Corrin	Design	25/4	Y	€198

1. Sort the database by date.
2. Print the first and last record in the database. (Hint: create a query that looks for the first or last surname.)
3. Search for artists who handed in work in April.
4. Search for artists who handed in work in April and who have not been paid yet.
5. Print the results of the search.
6. Add the following records to the database:

Your name	Design	25/5	N	€200
M Egan	Paint	21/5	N	€230

7. Create a new query to search for all the artists who have not been paid yet.
8. Print the ARTIST, DATE and FEE fields.
9. Sort the database by AREA.
10. Search for artists who are paid more than €150.
11. Print only the ARTIST, AREA and FEE fields for this search.
12. Save the database as POTTERY.

Rustic Pottery uses a spreadsheet to calculate the bonus due to an artist based on the number of sales of their pottery. An artist gets a 5% bonus at the end of each month, based on the total amount earned.

	A	B	C	D
1	Rustic Pottery Co.	Fee/Piece	€4.45	
2		Bonus	5%	
3	Artist Name	Pieces Sold	Fee	Bonus
4	J Gradowski	51		
5	D Brennan	34		
6	O Brougham	45		
7	P Jones	67		
8	A Sweeney	89		
9	S Kerr	23		
10	A Greir	45		
11	J Marin	54		
12	P Smith	65		
13	V Corrin	34		

1. Create the spreadsheet and insert a formula in cell C4 to calculate the fee earned by J Gradowski (multiply B4 by €4.45).
2. Copy the formula to the remaining cells in the column heading called Fee.
3. Insert a formula in cell D4 to calculate the bonus due to J Gradowski.
4. Copy the formula to the other cells in the column.
5. In cell A14, insert the word *Total*.
6. In cell B14, insert a function to calculate the total number of pieces sold. Copy this function to the other columns.
7. Save the file as POTTERY and print one copy.

Rustic Pottery has created a list of the items they stock for distribution to the various shops.

THE RUSTIC POTTERY Co.

Church Road, Oldcastle

Rustic Collection
Farmhouse Collection[1]
Rural Collection[2]
Old Time Collection

Each collection contains the following items:

1 teapot
6 cups and saucers
6 dinner plates
6 soup bowls
6 side dishes
6 dessert bowls
1 milk jug

We also stock:

vases
fruit bowls
lamps
clocks

[1] These items are unglazed.
[2] Will be available early next season.

1. Set a left margin of 1.5 inches and a right margin of 1 inch.
2. Put the company name and address in a header and centre it on the page.
3. Insert a footer as follows: 'Director Your Name'. Centre it on the page.
4. Use a proportional serif font for the letter.
5. Insert superscripts as shown.
6. Enhance the letter as appropriate.
7. Make the dinner set collection a numbered list.
8. Make the other items a bulleted list.
9. Save the file as POTTERY.
10. Print one copy.

Project 8

This project explores how IT is used in a busy restaurant. You use word processing to produce a menu for the restaurant. You see how a database can help in ordering food. You also use a spreadsheet to help calculate the running expenses.

Time The estimated time for this project is two hours.

Rating This project has a difficulty rating of two.

Skills You need the following skills to successfully complete this project:

Software Package	Tasks to Complete	Explanations (see pages)
Spreadsheet	Formatting, alignment	140
Database	Data entry form, queries, find/replace, sort	132, 136,
Word processing	Superscripts, bulleted list	127, 128

Project 8
_____
DATABASE

The Hungry Gullet Restaurant uses a database to hold information about its suppliers. The database contains the following fields:

FIELD	WIDTH	DATATYPE
NAME	10	Text
ADDRESS	12	Text
TEL	6	Numeric
PRODUCE	12	Text
QUANTITY	2	Numeric
DATE	8	Date
PAY	5	Text

The Hungry Gullet Ltd

NAME	————	TEL	————
ADDRESS	————	PRODUCE	————
QUANTITY	————	DATE	————
PAY	————		

Retrieve the database flie REST from the Web site. It contains the following information:

NAME	ADDRESS	TEL	PRODUCE	QUANTITY	DATE	PAY
Johnson	45 Will St	767432	Potatoes	24	12/4	COD
Johnson	45 Will St	767432	Carrots	5	13/4	COD
Laurence	12 Main St	423676	Onions	3	16/5	CASH
Timony	12 New Rd	556244	Potatoes	8	13/4	INV
Timony	12 New Rd	556224	Turnips	6	18/4	INV
Johnson	45 Will St	767432	Green Beans	6	12/5	COD
Laurence	12 Main St	423676	Garlic	1	25/4	CASH
Ferguson	Model Farm	664178	Pepper	2	28/4	CASH
Ferguson	Model Farm	664178	Spices	5	12/5	CASH
Laurence	12 Main St	423676	Herbs	4	25/4	CASH

1. Copy the database to your own drive.
2. Sort the database by supplier and save it as REST1.
3. Enhance the database as follows:
   • Put the NAME and PRODUCE fields in bold.
   • Put the PAY field in italics.
4. Search for suppliers who prefer being paid in cash.
5. Search for orders that are due in April.
6. Wentworth has bought Johnson. Make the necessary changes to the database.
7. Search for quantities of five or more that are due in May.
8. Save the updated database as REST2 and print one copy.

The Hungry Gullet uses spreadsheets to give a breakdown of the quarterly income and expenditure during the year. Create the following spreadsheet:

	A	B	C	D	E
1					
2	Income	1st Quarter	2nd Quarter	3rd Quarter	4th Quarter
3	Lunches	€3,446	€4,552	€3,885	€3,998
4	Evening Meal	€23,442	€26,688	€25,367	€28,447
5	Wine	€4,366	€4,988	€5,690	€5,130
6	Beer	€2,590	€2,709	€2,893	€2,488
7	Spirits	€2,788	€2,977	€2,688	€2,466
8					
9	Expenses				
10	Salaries	€16,500	€16,500	€16,500	€17,000
11	Rent	€3,200	€3,200	€3,200	€3,200
12	Electricity	€138	€126	€176	€129
13	Heating	€420	€480	€460	€490
14	Telephone	€368	€350	€456	€487
15	Advertising	€690	€690	€690	€780

1. Insert the word *Total* in cell A8. In cell B8, insert a formula to calculate the total income for the first quarter. Copy the formula to the other columns.
2. In cell A16, insert the word *Total*. In B16, insert a formula to calculate the total expenditure for the first quarter and copy it to the other columns.
3. In cell F2, insert the word *Total*. In F3, insert a formula to calculate the total income from lunches. Copy the formula to the other rows.
4. Insert the word *Profit* in A17. In cell B17, insert a formula to calculate the profit. Copy it to each column.
5. Make column A bold. Centre row two, and put it in italics.
6. Change the number values to currency values, which are accurate to two decimal places.
7. Save the file as REST and print one copy.

The restaurant wants to change its existing menu and make it more contemporary.

The Hungry Gullet Restaurant

Special Evening Dinner Menu

Starters
Caesar Salad
Crab Claws Coated with a Honey Mustard Dressing[1]
Soup de Jour
Garlic Mushrooms

Main Courses
Lobster Thermidor[1]
Salmon en Croûte
Beef Wellington
Noisette of Lamb
Chicken with a Cream/Dill/Garlic Sauce

Desserts
Ice Cream
Black Forest Gateau
Profiteroles
Death by Chocolate

Tea or Coffee

1. Set a left margin of 1.5 inches and a right margin of 1 inch.
2. Centre and underline the heading. Choose a contemporary font for the main headings.
3. Insert a line after each main heading.
4. Make the starters, main courses, and desserts bulleted lists. You can change the format of the bullets.
5. Insert the following words: *€32.00 for two before 8.00 p.m.* after the words *Special Evening Dinner Menu.*
6. Insert superscripts as shown.
7. On the final line, insert the superscript 1 with the following text: *When available fresh from market.*
8. Save the file as REST. Print one copy using your name as a footer.

Project 9

This project is set in a ferry company. You use the word processor to produce a schedule of sailing times. You will see how a database can help in scheduling sailing times. You also use a spreadsheet to calculate a fare.

Time   The estimated time for this project is two hours.

Rating   This project has a difficulty rating of two.

Skills   You need the following skills to successfully complete this project:

Software Package	Tasks to Complete	Explanations (see pages)
Spreadsheet	Formatting, alignment	140
Database	Data entry form, queries using AND, copy, insert field	132, 134, 136
Word processing	Margins, copy, bullets, formatting	125, 122, 128, 125

Project 9

DATABASE

The ferry company uses a database to hold information about its sailing times to various ports. The database contains the following fields:

FIELD	WIDTH	DATATYPE
DATE	8	Date
DAY	4	Text
DEPART	5	Numeric
ARRIVE	5	Numeric
FROM	10	Text
TO	12	Text

```
                    The Pixie Ferry Line
    DATE      _____      DAY       _____
    DEPART    _____      ARRIVE    _____
    FROM      _____      TO        _____
```

Retrieve the database FERRY from the Web site. It contains the following information:

DATE	DAY	DEPART	ARRIVE	FROM	TO
1/4	MON	09.00	16.30	DUBLIN	HOLYHEAD
1/4	MON	13.00	19.30	DUBLIN	HOLYHEAD
2/4	TUE	10.00	12.00	ROSSLARE	LE HAVRE
2/4	TUE	14.00	13.00	ROSSLARE	CHERBOURG
3/4	WED	08.00	14.30	BELFAST	LIVERPOOL
3/4	WED	12.00	15.30	LARNE	STRANRAER
4/4	THUR	13.00	01.00	ROSSLARE	PORTSMOUTH
4/4	THUR	17.00	22.00	DUBLIN	LIVERPOOL
5/4	FRI	07.00	09.00	ROSSLARE	LE HAVRE
6/4	SAT	09.00	08.00	ROSSLARE	CHERBOURG

1. Copy the database to your own drive.
2. Insert a new field called ARRDATE to hold details of the arrival date. Insert the following dates in this order:
   1/4, 1/4, 3/4, 3/4, 3/4, 3/4, 5/4, 4/4, 6/4 and 7/4.
   Change the data entry form to take account of the new field.
3. The 09.00 sailing from Dublin to Holyhead on 1 April has been cancelled. They plan to replace this sailing with one at 14.30, which will arrive at 21.30. Insert the new times.
4. A passenger phones to inquire about sailing from Rosslare to Cherbourg. What dates are available?
5. Another passenger wants to sail to France on Tuesday. What options are available?
6. Save the database as FERRY. Print one copy of the complete database.

Project 9
SPREADSHEET

The ferry company uses a spreadsheet to calculate the fare for a passenger. Create the following spreadsheet:

	A	B	C	D	E	F
1	PIXIE FERRY CO					
2	Rosslare to		High	Low	Number	Total
3	Cherbourg	Car + 4	€230	€180	0	
4		Adult	€70	€50	0	
5		Child	€35	€30	0	
6		OAP	€45	€40	0	
7		Student	€48	€42	0	
8						
9		Subtotal				
10		VAT			21%	
11		Total				

1. Insert a formula in cell F3 to multiply the number of cars and adults by the cost of the high-season fare.
2. Copy this formula to all the cells as far as F7. (The results will be zero, because you have not entered any numbers yet in column E.)
3. Insert a formula in F9 to add the range from F3 to F7.
4. Insert a formula in F10 to calculate the VAT applicable. In cell F11, insert a formula to calculate the total.
5. Calculate the fare for two adults, one child and one student.
6. Calculate the fare for one adult, three children and one old age pensioner (OAP).
7. Calculate the fare for a car with two passengers. (The fare for the car allows up to four passengers to travel. There is no discount for less than four passengers.)
8. Enhance the spreadsheet as appropriate.
9. Save the file as FERRY and print one copy.

The ferry company wants to draw up a schedule of sailing times. The following file (FERRY) is already in the database, so copy and paste it in the document:

PIXIE FERRY CO
12 Essex Street

The following are the sailing times for the week beginning 1 April and ending 8 April:

DATE	DAY	DEPART	ARRIVE	FROM	TO	ARRDATE
1/4	MON	14.30	21.30	DUBLIN	HOLYHEAD	1/4
1/4	MON	13.00	19.30	DUBLIN	LE HAVRE	1/4
2/4	TUE	10.00	12.00	ROSSLARE	CHERBOURG	3/4
2/4	TUE	14.00	13.00	ROSSLARE	LIVERPOOL	3/4
3/4	WED	08.00	14.30	BELFAST	LIVERPOOL	3/4
3/4	WED	12.00	15.30	LARNE	STRANRAER	3/4
4/4	THUR	13.00	01.00	ROSSLARE	PORTSMOUTH	5/4
4/4	THUR	17.00	22.00	DUBLIN	LIVERPOOL	4/4
5/4	FRI	07.00	09.00	ROSSLARE	LE HAVRE	6/4
6/4	SAT	09.00	08.00	ROSSLARE	CHERBOURG	7/4

On all our ferries, the restaurants offer à-la-carte meals. Cabins or reclining seats are available for overnight crossings.

Please phone prior to departure, because sailing may be delayed or cancelled due to weather conditions.

'A computer lets you make more mistakes faster than any invention in human history — with the possible exceptions of handguns and tequila.'
Mitch Ratliffe

1. Set a left margin of 1.25 inches and a right margin of 1.25 inches.
2. Centre and underline the heading. Choose a non-proportional font for the sailing dates and times.
3. Copy the data from the database and insert it after the first line as shown. (You may have to adjust the size of the text and align it properly.)
4. Make the last two paragraphs bulleted lists.
5. Enhance the document as follows:
   • Make the Date column bold.
   • Put the From and To columns in italics.
6. Save the file as FERRY and print one copy. Type your name as a footer.

Project 10

This project is set in an airline. The airline uses word processing to produce an advertisement. You will see how a database can help to schedule flying times. You will also use a spreadsheet to help calculate fares.

Time   The estimated time for this project is two hours.

Rating   This project has a difficulty rating of two.

Skills   You need the following skills to successfully complete this project:

Software Package	Tasks to Complete	Explanations (see pages)
Spreadsheet	Formatting	140
Database	Data entry form, queries	132, 134
Word processing	Margins, superscripts, bulleted list	125, 127, 128

Project 10

DATABASE

The airline uses many databases e.g. to track passengers, flights and employees etc. In this project, the airline uses a database to track flights for a single day. The database consists of the following fields:

FIELD NAME	WIDTH	DATATYPE
CODE	7	Numeric
DEPART	10	Text
ARRIVE	10	Text
DTIME	4	Time
ATIME	4	Time

'Cannot find

REALITY.SYS...

Universe halted.'

Anon

Create a data entry form similar to the following:

The OK Airline Co.			
CODE	_____	DEPART	_____
ARRIVE	_____	DTIME	_____
ATIME	_____		

Retrieve the database AIRLINE from the Web site. It contains the following information:

CODE	DEPART	ARRIVE	DTIME	ATIME
EI 1233	DUBLIN	LONDON	08.00	09.30
BA 3455	DUBLIN	ROME	08.30	13.00
BA 3321	LONDON	DUBLIN	08.00	09.30
EI 5433	LONDON	DUBLIN	08.25	09.55
AP 8832	LISBON	DUBLIN	10.35	14.55
LA 3362	DUBLIN	BERLIN	09.45	12.45
AF 4436	PARIS	DUBLIN	12.00	14.35
AI 2274	DUBLIN	ROME	13.00	17.30
EI 8823	DUBLIN	LONDON	14.30	16.00
EI 3833	BERLIN	DUBLIN	15.00	18.05

1. Copy the database to your own drive and save it as FLIGHT.
2. Enhance the database as follows:
   • Make the CODE field bold.
   • Put the DEPART and DTIME fields in italics.
   • Change the font on the ARRIVE and ATIME fields.
3. The flight LA 3362 from Dublin to Berlin has been cancelled. Remove this row.

4. Insert the following two flights:

EI 8773	DUBLIN	ROME	16.30	21.00
EI 3266	DUBLIN	BELFAST	16.00	17.05

5. Search for all flights departing from Dublin.
6. Search for all flights from Dublin to London.
7. Flight AP 8832 from Lisbon to Dublin is running thirty minutes behind schedule. Update the database as appropriate.
8. Search for all Aer Lingus flights. The code begins with the letters *EI*.
9. Print a copy of the complete database.

The airline uses spreadsheets to calculate fares and wages etc. The spreadsheet will be used to calculate the return fare between Dublin and London, based on factors such as age, excess baggage etc. Create the following spreadsheet:

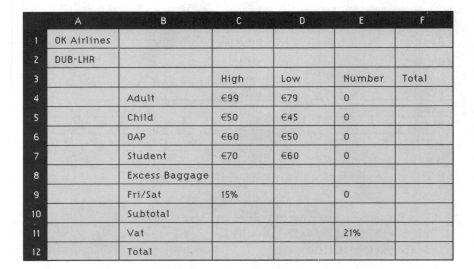

	A	B	C	D	E	F
1	OK Airlines					
2	DUB-LHR					
3			High	Low	Number	Total
4		Adult	€99	€79	0	
5		Child	€50	€45	0	
6		OAP	€60	€50	0	
7		Student	€70	€60	0	
8		Excess Baggage				
9		Fri/Sat	15%		0	
10		Subtotal				
11		Vat			21%	
12		Total				

1. Insert a formula in cell F4 to multiply the number of adults by the cost of the high-season fare.
2. Copy this formula as far as cell F7. (All the results will be zero, because you have not entered any numbers yet in column E.).
3. In cell F8, insert a formula to calculate the penalty for excess baggage. This will be the number in cell E8 multiplied by 1.5.
4. Insert a formula in cell F9 to calculate whether a 15% surcharge on weekend flights will apply. (Hint: add the contents of F4 to F7, multiply by C9, and then multiply by E9. If there is a flight on Friday or Saturday, then E9 will have a value of one [1], otherwise it will have a value of zero [0].)
5. Insert a formula in cell F10 to calculate the subtotal.
6. Insert a formula in cell F11 to calculate the VAT that is applicable. In F12, insert a formula to calculate the total.
7. Calculate the fare for two adults and two children travelling at the weekend. Now recalculate the fare, assuming an excess baggage of 12kg.
8. Save the file as AIRLINE and print one copy.

The airline company wants to recruit new cabin staff using the following advertisement:

OK AIRLINES

Do you want a high-flying career? If so, you should talk to us. Due to expansion in the European market, we are currently recruiting cabin and ground staff.

We offer:

A comprehensive training programme
Attractive salary
Medical insurance
Bonus Loyalty Shares each year
Promotional opportunities
Free Travel

We Seek:

Male and female candidates, aged between 18 and 30
Fluency in a European language
Good personal grooming and appearance
Height between 5 feet 5 inches and 6 feet[1]
Interested? Send a CV to Margery at OK Airlines.

1. Set a left margin of 1.25 inches and a right margin of 1.25 inches.
2. Centre and underline the heading. Make the heading size 18 points.
3. Make the font size in the first paragraph 14 points.
4. Put the words *We Offer* and *We Seek* in bold.
5. Format the list items as bulleted lists.
6. Insert the superscript as shown. Insert the following line, at the bottom of the document: [1] *Height restrictions apply only to Cabin Staff.*
7. Centre the last line.
8. Insert your name as a footer and print one copy.
9. Save the file as AIRLINE.

Project 11

This project is set in a factory that produces candles. The factory uses IT in its everyday activities. It uses IT in the following ways:
- Spreadsheets to calculate the company payroll
- Databases to store data about its clients
- Word processing for internal documents, external letters and reports

Time   The estimated time for this project is two hours.

Rating   This project has a difficulty rating of two.

Skills   You need the following skills to successfully complete this project:

Software Package	Tasks to Complete	Explanations (see pages)
Spreadsheet	Insert row	140
Database	Using mathematics on fields, multilevel sorting, queries, copy	135, 133, 134
Word processing	Margins, numbered list	125, 128

Project 11
DATABASE

The factory uses a database to track customers and orders etc. The database has the following structure:

FIELD NAME	WIDTH	DATATYPE
NAME	15	Text
ORDERNO	5	Alphanumeric
DATE	8	Date
DESCRIPTION	20	Text
QUANTITY	1	Numeric
PRICE	6	Currency

Create a data entry form similar to the following:

```
                    The Lux Candle Co.
    NAME      _____      ORDERNO     _____
    DATE      _____      DESCRIPTION _____
    QUANTITY  _____      PRICE       _____
```

Retrieve the database file CANDLE from the Web site. It contains the following information:

NAME	ORDERNO	DATE	DESCRIPTION	QUANTITY	PRICE
FLOOD	A1134	12/7	White, scented	5	€14.50
JOHNSON	A1135	13/7	White, scented	4	€14.50
O' HARA	A1145	14/7	Beeswax, unscented	4	€20.00
MCELWEE	B1155	19/6	Beeswax, scented	3	€18.00
MCCALLUM	B1157	12/6	Blue, unscented	3	€14.50
SWEENEY	A1136	18/7	Marbled, unscented	5	€15.50
GRIER	B1156	13/6	Blue, scented	3	€15.50
KERR	C2290	23/7	Marbled, scented	4	€16.00
MARTIN	B1154	21/6	White, scented	6	€14.50
FIRTH	C2291	22/7	White, scented	4	€14.50

1. Copy the database to your own drive and save it as CANDLE.
2. Insert a new field called TOTAL. Insert a formula to multiply the QUANTITY field by the PRICE field.
3. Enhance the database as follows:
   • Make the NAME and TOTAL fields bold.
   • Put the DESCRIPTION field in italics.
4. Remove FLOOD from the supplier list.
5. Insert the following records:

DOHERTY	B1160	22/6	White, scented	5	€14.50
O'LOONEY	C2292	19/7	White, unscented	3	€13.50

6. Sort the database using the ORDERNO field.
7. Search for orders for white, scented candles.
8. Search for orders worth more than €60.00.
9. Sort the database using the ORDERNO field as the primary field and the DATE field as the secondary field.
10. Insert a new field called VAT and insert a formula to calculate the VAT on the TOTAL field at 21%.
11. Print one copy and save the file as CANDLE.

The candle factory uses spreadsheets in the payroll department. The pension contributions are given for each employee. Create the spreadsheet as follows:

	A	B	C	D	E	F	G	H
1	LUX Candles			Tax Rate 24%	Pension 5%			
2								
3	Employee	Hours	Rate	Gross	Pension	Taxable	Tax	Net
4	Prendergast	39	€12.00					
5	Morgan	41	€12.00					
6	Adler	42	€14.00					
7	Royce	38	€10.50					
8	Jones	35	€7.80					
9	Ferry	39	€12.00					

1. Insert a formula in cell D4 to calculate the gross salary for Prendergast. Copy the formula to the other rows.
2. In cell E4, insert a formula to calculate the pension contribution for Prendergast. Copy the formula to the other rows.
3. Insert a formula in F4 to subtract the pension contribution from the gross salary to determine the taxable income. Copy the formula to the other rows.
4. In cell G4, insert a formula to calculate the amount of tax payable (24% of the value in F4). Copy the formula to the other rows.
5. Insert a formula in cell H4 to calculate the net salary. Copy the formula to the other rows.
6. Insert a row between rows 6 and 7 and enter the following data: Your name, working 39 hours at a rate of €12.00 per hour.
7. Copy the formulas to the new row.
8. Save the file as CANDLE and print one copy.

The candle factory uses word processing for internal and external documents. The following document is for internal circulation as a company newsletter:

LUX CANDLES

Week beginning

Well done to all who participated at the weekend BBQ! It was a great success. Special thanks to Ivor and Shane who organised the whole day.

Next week, Noreen and Dymphna have organised a paintball game on Saturday from 2.00 p.m. to 5.30 p.m. They want as many as possible to turn up for a great day's shooting!

Congratulations to Mary and Kevin on the birth of their baby boy (also called Kevin).

Worker of the week was a tie between Eithne and Martin (brother and sister)! The prize as usual is a half-day on Friday. Enjoy!

The safety inspector (Caroline) has asked me to point out that there will be a safety audit this Thursday. Enquiries to Ext 335.

The computer department has asked me to point out that viruses are becoming a major problem, mainly through contaminated e-mail.
Please make sure that your PC has an up-to-date virus scanner.

'Scandisk is now checking your hard disk. You can start praying.'

Anon

1. Set a left margin of 1.25 inches and a right margin of 1.25 inches.
2. Centre and underline the heading. Choose a non-proportional font and make it size 16. Use the computer to automatically insert the dates.
3. Use a proportional font, size 12, for the rest of the bulletin.
4. Make each paragraph a numbered list.
5. Enhance as follows:
   • Make the first word of each list item bold.
   • Put the first names in italics.
6. Insert your name as a footer. Save the file as CANDLE and print one copy.

Project 12

This project explores how IT is used in a bank. Apart from the obvious use of spreadsheets, banks use word processing to write letters to clients. They use databases to access client records, for example, their credit rating etc.

Time   The estimated time for this project is two hours.

Rating   This project has a difficulty rating of two.

Skills   You need the following skills to successfully complete this project:

Software Package	Tasks to Complete	Explanations (see pages)
Spreadsheet	Formatting	140
Database	Using mathematics on fields, sorting, queries	135, 132, 134
Word processing	Copy, enhance	122, 125

Project 12
DATABASE

The bank uses a database to track customers and to access credit ratings etc. The database has the following structure:

FIELD NAME	WIDTH	DATATYPE
NAME	10	Text
ADDRESS	15	Text
ACCOUNT NO	9	Numeric
BALANCE	8	Currency
LOAN	8	Currency
CREDIT	1	Numeric

Create a data entry form similar to the following:

The Treasury Bank of Westpool		
NAME _____	ADDRESS _____	
ACCOUNT NO _____	BALANCE _____	
LOAN _____	CREDIT _____	

Retrieve the database file BANK from the Web site. It contains the following information:

NAME	ADDRESS	ACCOUNT NO	BALANCE	LOAN	CREDIT
Tompkins	45 Will St	223244456	+€34,500	€2,000	1
Wilson	45 Will St	224677889	+€22,400	€3,500	2
Worth	12 Main St	664443362	+€10,500	0	2
Black	12 New Rd	556732217	+€4,800	€2,000	4
Penny	12 New Rd	242477224	+€7,890	0	3
Jones	45 Will St	166427767	+€900	0	5
Smith	12 Main St	356334567	-€1,499	€2,000	7
Williams	14 East St	241678124	-€1,099	€1,000	7
Warner	22 Old Rd	488675933	-€3,400	€4,000	8
Egan	12 South St	266533743	+€1,200	0	4

1. Copy the database to your own drive and save it as BANK.
2. Enhance the database as follows:
   • Make the NAME field bold.
   • Make the BALANCE field bold.
   • Put the LOAN field in italics.
   • Change the font in the CREDIT field.
3. Remove the record for Worth.
4. Sort the database by NAME.
5. Insert the following two records in their correct positions:

West	23 New Rd	468558933	+€3,400	€4,000	5
Your name	13 South St	264432743	+€1,800	0	4

6. The credit rating goes from one (excellent) to eight (poor). Search for a rating of four or less.
7. Add a new field called TOTAL, and insert a formula to subtract the loan from the balance.
8. Account no. 488675933 wants a loan. Check the credit rating.
9. Print one copy of the complete database.

Project 12

SPREADSHEET

The bank uses spreadsheets to calculate the interest payable on overdrafts on a monthly basis. Interest is charged on the highest amount that the account was overdrawn in that month. Set up the following spreadsheet:

	A	B	C	D	E
1	Your Name				
2	From 1/3/00	To 31/3/00			
3	Account	1522469			
4	Date	Transaction	Debit	Credit	Balance
5	1/3/00	Balance			€1,200
6	3/3/00	Lodgment		€200	
7	12/3/00	CHK 0099033	− €300		
8	18/3/00	CHK 9983332	− €1,400		
9	23/3/00	ATM withdrawal, Westpool	− €1,200		
10	24/3/00	CHK 0099034		€300	
11	28/3/00	Lodgment		€400	
12	29/3/00	CHK 3342232		€900	

1. Format the Credit, Debit and Balance columns as currency values, which are accurate to two decimal places.
2. Insert a formula in cell E6 to calculate the balance. (Hint: it will be the sum of E5 plus the credit and debit amount for 3 March 2000.) Copy this formula to the other cells in column E.
3. Interest is charged at a rate of 17% on the highest amount overdrawn during the month. In cell B13, insert the word *Highest*. In cell E13, insert a function to calculate the highest amount overdrawn during the month (use the MIN function).
4. In cell B14, insert *Interest @ 17%*. In cell E14, insert a function to determine the interest payable on the amount in E13. Divide this amount by twelve to find the monthly interest.
5. Enhance the spreadsheet as appropriate and print one copy.
6. Save the file as BANK.

A customer has asked the bank for a statement, because she is concerned at the high rate of interest she is being charged. In this part of the project, you will draft a letter to the customer and insert a copy of her bank statement, created in the spreadsheet section.

The Treasury Bank of Westpool

Date

Dear Name,

Further to your enquiry regarding your overdraft, I enclose this month's statement. The bank has arranged an overdraft facility for you for €3,000. The interest charged on this is 17%.

Your Name
From 1/3/00   To 30/3/00
Account 1522469

Date	Transaction	Debit	Credit	Balance
1/3/00	Balance			€1,200.00
3/3/00	Lodgment		€200.00	€1,400.00
12/3/00	CHK 0099033	– €300.00		€1,100.00
18/3/00	CHK 9983332	– €1,400.00		– €300.00
23/3/00	ATM withdrawal, Westpool	– €1,200.00		– €1,500.00
24/3/00	CHK 0099034		€300.00	– €1,200.00
28/3/00	Lodgment		€400.00	– €800.00
29/3/00	CHK 3342232		€900.00	€100.00
	HIGHEST			**– €1,500.00**
	Interest@17%			**€21.25**

Perhaps a personal loan would suit your needs better. We offer competitive rates of 8.5% (APR 9.2%). If you would like to drop in to discuss terms, I would be delighted to arrange a time convenient for both of us.

Sincerely,

1. Create the previous letter and insert the spreadsheet data.
2. Enhance the letter as you see fit.
3. Print one copy and save the letter as BANK.

Project 13

This project is set in a solicitor's office. You will be required to create a document with form fields, using a word processor. It will be a standard letter of reply with fields for the date etc. You will also interrogate a database of clients, and create a spreadsheet that calculates the cost of a case.

Time   The estimated time for this project is one and one-half hours.

Rating   This project has a difficulty rating of three.

Skills   You need the following skills to successfully complete this project:

Software Package	Tasks to Complete	Explanations (see pages)
Spreadsheet	Formatting	140
Database	Index, query	136, 134
Word processing	Form fields	129

Project 13

DATABASE

LegalEagles have created a database using the following fields:

• Name — Indicates the name of the client
• Address — Indicates the full address
• Tel — Indicates the telephone number
• Instruction — Indicates the date that the firm received instructions from the client
• Nature — Indicates the type of case
• Brief — Indicates the name of the barrister taking the case
• Court — Indicates the date (if any) that the case is due to be heard in court

FIELD NAME	WIDTH	DATATYPE
NAME	10	Text
ADDRESS	15	Text
TEL	7	Numeric
INSTRUCTION	8	Date
NATURE	10	Text
BRIEF	10	Text
COURT	8	Date

Retrieve the database file LEGAL from the Web site. It contains the following information:

NAME	ADDRESS	TEL	INST	NATURE	BRIEF	COURT
Smith	12 East St		12/2/99	Will	N/A	N/A
Bradley	23 Main St		15/7/98	Accident	Kelly	2/1/00
Adams	12 Main St		9/8/99	Will	N/A	N/A
Jones	2 Old Rd		4/5/97	Accident	Kelly	13/4/99
Craig	4 New Rd		13/2/99	Robbery	Marks	9/5/00
Kelly	45 Will St		16/7/98	Will	N/A	N/A
Rogers	28 Gray St		19/7/98	Accident	Kelly	12/3/00
Savage	1 Park St		13/2/99	Will	N/A	N/A
Kent	56 West St		23/7/99	Robbery	Marks	17/2/00
Martin	23 East St		13/8/99	Theft	Marks	18/2/00

1. Insert the telephone numbers.
2. Create an index on the INSTRUCTION field and call it INST.
3. Insert the following two new records in their correct positions:

Smith	23 West St		13/9/99	Accident	Kelly	18/3/00
Your Name	3 West St		14/10/99	Accident	Kelly	28/4/00

4. Print the first and last records of the database.
5. Jones's case has been settled out of court. Remove this record from the database.
6. Assuming today's date is 21 January 2000, search for cases that still have to come before the courts. (Hint: search under the COURT field for dates greater than 21 January 2000.)
7. Search for cases where Kelly has the brief and print the results.
8. Search for cases where Marks has the brief and print only the NAME, NATURE and COURT fields.
9. Save the database as LEGAL.

LegalEagles use a spreadsheet to calculate the cost of a case, based on the nature of the case, the hours worked and the financial value of the case. Create the following spreadsheet:

	A	B	C	D	E
1	Case No A-dd334			No.	Total
2		Fee/Hour	€16.00	0	
3		Case Value		0	
4		Personal Injury	10%	0	
5		Conveyancing	2%	0	
6		Probate	€600	0	
7		Criminal		0	
8		Subtotal			
9		Vat @ 21%			
10		Total			

'Press any key…

no, no, no, NOT

THAT ONE!'

Anon

The case value is calculated as follows:

1. In cell E2, insert a formula to multiply the fee per hour by the hours worked. (The answer will be zero, because you have not entered any hours yet.)
2. In cell E4, calculate 10% of the case value and multiply this by the value in D4. (Cell D4 contains the value one [1] if it is a personal injury case, or zero [0] if it is another type of case.) Insert a similar formula in cell E5.
3. Insert a formula in E6 to calculate the fee for probate. (Hint: multiply the value in C6 by D6. The value one [1] signifies that the case is probate, the value zero [0] signifies that it is another type of case.)
4. In cell E7, multiply C7 (the number of hours) by the fee per hour.
5. In cell E8, insert a function to add the contents of E2 to E7.
6. In cell E9, insert a formula to add VAT at 21%.
7. Insert a formula to calculate the total in E10.
8. Use this spreadsheet to calculate the fee for the following:
   • Personal injury, settled for €34,900
   • Sale of a house for €120,500
   • A criminal case where the number of hours worked was twelve
9. Save the file as LEGAL and print one copy.

LegalEagles have standard letters on file which use form fields to enter information e.g. client name, date etc. Create the following letter using form fields:

LegalEagles Ltd
LegalEagle House
Limerick

DOCTOR NAME
ADDRESS 1
ADDRESS 2
ADDRESS 3

Date

Dear DOCTOR NAME,

We are representing our client, CLIENT NAME, who we believe has sustained injury in the workplace. We would be grateful if you could prepare a medical report detailing the injuries.

We look forward to hearing from you shortly.

Yours sincerely,

I G Allen
Solicitor

1. Save the letter as LEGAL.
2. Insert today's date.
3. Insert your own name and address in the DOCTOR NAME field.
4. Use a friend's name in the CLIENT NAME field.
5. Print one copy of the document.
6. Use the document to print another letter using the following information:
   • Dr Muriel Kilroy, 12 Main Street, Oldcastle, Co. Donegal.
   • The client's name is John Cooper.
7. Print a copy of the letter.

Project 14

This project is set in a travel agency. You must create a document with form fields, using a word processor. It will be a standard letter of reply with fields for the date etc. You will also interrogate a database and create a spreadsheet that calculates the cost of a holiday.

Time The estimated time for this project is two hours.

Rating This project has a difficulty rating of three.

Skills You need the following skills to successfully complete this project:

Software Package	Tasks to Complete	Explanations (see pages)
Spreadsheet	Formatting	140
Database	Index, copying records, query	136, 134
Word processing	Form fields	129

Project 14
DATABASE

The travel agency uses a number of different databases.

FIELD NAME	WIDTH	DATATYPE
NAME	10	Text
DESTINATION	12	Text
DATE	8	Date
FLIGHT_NO	6	Alphanumeric
DEPART	5	Numeric
ARRIVE	5	Numeric

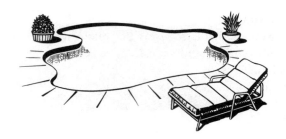

Retrieve the file TRAVEL1 from the Web site. This is a simplified version of an actual database, which a travel agent might use. Copy the five records in the database. Open the file TRAVEL2, and insert the five records into the file. You now have a database that contains the following ten records:

NAME	DESTINATION	DATE	FLIGHT NO	DEPART	ARRIVE
Saunders	Salou	12/4/00	EI 122	17.45	20.30
Jones	Tenerife	14/5/00	AE 133	13.00	16.50
Peters	Athens	24/3/00	DA 332	23.00	3.45
Foster	Nice	27/6/00	AF 91	11.45	13.50
King	Miami	13/3/00	BA 23	10.35	16.30
Black	Kos	14/4/00	DA 22	14.50	20.00
Adams	Corfu	23/4/00	DA 221	17.45	23.45
Brophy	Paris	29/8/00	AF 252	13.00	15.30
Mitchell	New York	16/7/00	TA 332	15.45	21.30
Taunton	Miami	25/6/00	BA 111	12.40	18.40

1. Create an index on the DATE field and call it DATE.
2. Add the following two records:

Kent	Paris	25/6/00	AF 223	12.45	15.00
Wilson	Nice	29/8/00	BA 422	10.30	12.35

3. Search for flights to France. (Hint: the destination contains Nice or Paris.) Print the results of this search.
4. Print only the NAME, DATE, DEPART and ARRIVE fields.
5. Mr Foster telephones to double-check the departure and arrival times. Retrieve the record containing this information.
6. Search for morning flights only.
7. Search for Air France flights (the code contains AF).
8. Create a new index on the FLIGHT NO field and call it FLIGHT.
9. Print the following fields: NAME, DESTINATION and FLIGHT NO.
10. Save the file as TRAVEL3.

Project 14

SPREADSHEET

This spreadsheet calculates the cost of a holiday, based on the number of weeks, the number of people etc. Create the following spreadsheet:

	A	B	C	D
1	AWOL Holidays Ltd			
2		No. of Weeks		
3		Cost/Week		
4		No. of Persons		
5		Supplements		
6		Insurance		
7				
8		Subtotal		
9		Vat ⍺ 21%		
10		Total		
11				

You must insert a formula in cell C8 to calculate the cost of the holiday, based on the number of weeks, the number of persons etc. The formula is as follows:

Subtotal = (No. of Weeks * Cost/Week * No. of persons) + (Supplements * No. of people) + (Insurance * No. of people)

1. Calculate the cost of a holiday for four persons, who will be on holidays for two weeks at a cost of €450 per week for each person. There are no supplements and insurance is €30 per person. Print the results of the calculation.
2. Calculate the cost of a holiday for two persons for one week at a cost of €550 per week for each person. The supplements cost €25.00 per person. The insurance costs €20 per person. Print the results of the calculation.
3. Calculate the cost of a holiday for three persons for three weeks at a cost of €550 per week for each person. There are no supplements to be paid. The insurance costs €35 per person. Print the results.
4. Save the file as TRAVEL and print it.

AWOL Holidays have created some standard letters for replying to customer queries. One of the letters, which uses form fields, is shown below. Create the letter.

AWOL Holidays Ltd.
AWOL House
Main Street
Eastcourt

<NAME>
<ADDRESS1>
<ADDRESS2>
<ADDRESS3>

DATE

Dear <NAME>,

Thank you for inquiring about holidays in <DESTINATION>.

I have pleasure in enclosing our new <SEASON> brochure for <YEAR>, which I'm sure you will find appealing.

When you choose your holiday, please contact me and I will arrange all the necessary details.

Sincerely,

'Bad Command or File Name. Good try though.'

Anon

1. Save the letter as HOLIDAY.
2. Use this letter to produce a letter for each of the following people:
   - M Firth, 274 Knockbreda Road, Belfast enquiring about holidays in Thailand in the spring of 2001.
   - L West, 221 John St, Milford, enquiring about holidays in South Africa in the summer of 2001.
   - E Holly, 9 Main St, Oldcastle enquiring about holidays in Austria in the winter of 2001.
3. Save each letter as HOL1, HOL2 and HOL3.
4. Enhance the letters as appropriate.
5. Sign the letters with your name. Print one of them.

Project 15

This project, which is set in an architect's office, looks at how form fields are used in word processing to simplify standard letters. In the database section, you see how indexing a database can improve its efficiency. Finally in the spreadsheet section, you see how spreadsheets can calculate the payroll.

Time   The estimated time for this project is two hours.

Rating   This project has a difficulty rating of three.

Skills   You need the following skills to successfully complete this project:

Software Package	Tasks to Complete	Explanations (see pages)
Spreadsheet	Formatting, chart	140
Database	Index, copying records	136
Word processing	Form fields	129

Project 15

DATABASE

The architect uses a database to track customers, project costs, and whether clients have paid their bills. The database contains the following fields:

- NAME — Customer name
- CONTRACTOR — Name of the contractor
- START_DATE — Date the project started
- FINISH_DATE — Completion date of the project
- COST — Estimated total cost of the project
- FEE — Architect's fee
- PAID — Whether the architect was paid or not

FIELD NAME	WIDTH	DATATYPE
NAME	12	Text
CONTRACTOR	10	Text
START_DATE	8	Date
FINISH_DATE	8	Date
COST	5	Currency
FEE	7	Currency
PAID	1	Yes/No

Retrieve the file ARCH from the Web site. Copy the five records to the file ARCH1. The database now contains the following ten records:

NAME	CONTRACTOR	START_DATE	FINISH_DATE	COST (millions)	FEE	PAID
Saunders	Jones	12/3/99	23/4/00	€1.5	€25,000	N
Mitchell	PPK	14/5/00	19/5/02	€2.3	€40,300	N
Peters	Jones	22/3/99	23/5/00	€0.89	€17,500	N
Foster	Menton	25/6/00	16/4/02	€2.4	€43,000	N
King	PPK	30/1/00	12/5/01	€1.34	€22,000	N
Black	Menton	26/7/00	15/7/03	€3.45	€73,400	Y
Kelly	PPK	7/8/00	19/3/03	€3.24	€73,200	N
Timms	Jones	23/8/99	8/2/01	€2.12	€38,000	Y
Ferry	Menton	15/6/99	14/5/02	€4.56	€93,500	N
Taunton	PPK	23/9/00	19/3/02	€2.34	€42,800	Y

1. Create an index on the START_DATE field and call it START.
2. Add the following two records:

Timms	Jones	14/7/02	23/5/04	€2.13	€39,000	N
Your name	PPK	13/5/01	12/8/02	€1.56	€23,400	N

3. Print the first and last record of the database.
4. Search for projects that are due to be completed by 31 December 2001 and have not been paid for.
5. Print the results of the search.
6. Search for projects costing €3 million or more.
7. Create a new index on the CONTRACTOR field.
8. Search for fees of €50,000 or more.
9. Print only the NAME, CONTRACTOR and FEE fields for this search.
10. Create a new search for unpaid fees worth more than €50,000.
11. Print the NAME, CONTRACTOR, FEE and PAID fields for unpaid fees worth more than €50,000.
12. Save the file as ARCH2.

Project 15

SPREADSHEET

This spreadsheet calculates the overtime due to each architect, based on the number of hours worked each week during one month. Create the following spreadsheet:

	A	B	C	D	E	F
1	J Martin Architects		Cost/Hr 1	€12.00		
2			Cost/Hr 2	€16.00		
3	Name	N Daly	K Jones	M Peters	B Barton	Total
4	Week 1	40	45	50	43	
5	Week 2	40	43	42	46	
6	Week 3	43	40	50	42	
7	Week 4	40	40	50	45	
8	Total					
9	Overtime					
10	Cost of Overtime					

1. Insert a formula in cell B8 to calculate the total number of hours worked.
2. Copy this formula to the cells in the other columns.
3. In cell B9, insert a formula to calculate the number of overtime hours worked (i.e. more than 160 hours per month).
4. Copy the formula to the cells in the other columns.
5. Daly and Jones are on fee structure one; that is, they are paid €12.00 per hour. Peters and Barton are on fee structure two; that is, they are paid €16.00 per hour. In cell B10, insert a formula to calculate the cost of overtime. (Overtime = 1.5 × normal rate)
6. Create a chart showing the amount of overtime each employee generates in this four-week period.
7. Print the spreadsheet and the chart.
8. Save the file as ARCH.

J Martin Architects use standard letters, especially when applying for planning permission on behalf of clients. Create the following letter, using the form fields specified:

> <NAME>
> <ADDRESS1>
> <ADDRESS2>
> <ADDRESS3>
>
> DATE
>
> To Whom It May Concern,
>
> I <NAME> am applying for <TYPE> planning permission to erect a <NUMBER> storey dwelling house at <ADDRESS4>. The full plans can be inspected at the county council offices.
>
> Signed
>
> NAME

1. Using the previous letter, print two letters using the following information:
   - Letter 1 — John Smith, 23 Gray Street, Brentford is applying for full planning permission to erect a single-storey building at 2 Old Lane, Brentford.
   - Letter 2 — Sarah Ford, 2 Castlefield Road, Greenford is applying for outline-planning permission to erect a two-storey dwelling at 4 New Road, Greenford.
2. Enhance the letters as appropriate.
3. Print both letters.
4. Save the letters as ARCH1 and ARCH2.

'Warning: Keyboard not attached. Press F10 to continue.'

Anon

Project 16

A leisure centre uses IT applications in the following ways:

- Word processing — To create flyers and import clip art to advertise upcoming events
- Database — To create a schedule of times during each week when the centre is used
- Spreadsheets — To analyse the day-to-day expenses

Time   The estimated time for this project is two hours.

Rating   This project has a difficulty rating of three.

Skills   You need the following skills to successfully complete this project:

Software Package	Tasks to Complete	Explanations (see pages)
Spreadsheet	Insert rows/columns, formatting, chart	140
Database	Index, find/replace	136
Word processing	Importing clip art	122

Project 16

DATABASE

You are required to create a database for the Westpool Leisure Centre. Create a database using the following fields:

- Day — Day of booking
- Time — Time of booking
- Activity — Name of activity being booked
- Instructor — Course instructor
- Cost — Cost of booking
- Duration — Duration of course

FIELD NAME	WIDTH	DATATYPE
DAY	9	Text
TIME	12	Numeric
ACTIVITY	12	Text
INSTRUCTOR	10	Text
COST	5	Currency
DURATION	10	Text

Insert the following records and save the file as LEISURE:

TIME	DAY	ACTIVITY	INSTRUCTOR	COST	DURATION
6.30 - 8.00	Monday	Swimming 1	Cash	€40.00	10 weeks
6.30 - 8.00	Tuesday	Lifesaving 1	Green	€35.00	12 weeks
8.00 - 9.30	Monday	Lifesaving 2	Green	€40.00	15 weeks
6.00 - 8.00	Tuesday	Weights 1	Fullerton	€50.00	10 weeks
6.00 - 8.00	Thursday	Circuits 1	Menton	€35.00	8 weeks
8.00 - 10.00	Thursday	Get Fit	Barton	€35.00	8 weeks
2.00 - 3.00	Saturday	Get Fitter	Barton	€35.00	10 weeks
2.00 - 4.00	Saturday	Swimming 2	Cash	€45.00	12 weeks
6.00 - 8.00	Wednesday	Weights 2	Fullerton	€50.00	12 weeks
8.00 - 9.30	Wednesday	Circuits 2	Menton	€35.00	10 weeks

1. Create an index using a suitable field.
2. A customer phones to inquire about swimming classes. List the swimming classes available.
3. Ferguson has replaced the instructor Barton. Make the necessary adjustments.
4. Another customer asks for classes costing less than €40.00. Print a list of these classes.
5. Yet another customer phones to inquire about swimming classes on either a Monday or a Saturday. List the classes that fulfil these criteria.
6. Add another two classes to the database. Insert the records as follows:

6.00 - 8.00	Wednesday	Swimming 1	Cash	€50.00	10 weeks
8.00 - 9.30	Monday	Circuits 1	Menton	€35.00	8 weeks

7. Sort the database by the DAY field and then by the TIME field.
8. Repeat the queries in questions two and four.
9. Print only the DAY, TIME, ACTIVITY and COST fields.
10. Print one copy of the complete database.

Project 16
SPREADSHEET

The leisure centre uses the spreadsheet to calculate the running expenses on a quarterly basis. Create the following spreadsheet:

	A	B	C	D	E	F
1						
2		Jan	Feb	Mar	Apr	Total
3	Turnover	€12,540	€13,400	€12,670	€13,250	
4	Electricity	€1,130	€1,100	€1,080	€1,040	
5	Heating	€460	€480	€470	€485	
6	Mortgage	€2,500	€2,500	€2,500	€2,500	
7	Wages	€5,490	€5,490	€5,490	€5,490	
8	Cleaning	€450	€450	€450	€450	
9	Profit					
10	Per cent					

1. In cell F3, insert a function to calculate the total turnover for the first quarter.
2. Copy this function to the other rows.
3. In cell B9, insert a formula to calculate the profit for January (turnover minus the sum of expenses).
4. Copy this formula to the cells for the other months.
5. Align the months to the right of each cell, and make the headings in column A bold.
6. Enhance the spreadsheet as you see fit.
7. Create a chart showing the relationships between the expenses only.
8. Print one copy of the chart.
9. Format row ten as a percentage to one decimal place.
10. In cell B10, insert a formula to calculate the profit as a percentage of the turnover.
11. Insert a blank row between rows two and three, and another row between *Cleaning* and *Profit*.
12. Insert a blank column between *April* and *Total*.
13. Print one copy of the spreadsheet.
14. Save the file as LEISURE.

The leisure centre wants to create a flyer for door-to-door distribution in the immediate locality. The manager wants to create a picture to include in the flyer. Create a graphic for the logo in a software-painting package and import it into the flyer:

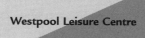

Westpool Leisure Centre

Welcome to Westpool Leisure Centre. We are offering some very special deals to help you stay fit and healthy this summer. Take a look at the following:

Weights — Join our customised weights-training programme with your own personal trainer. We will assess you and build a comprehensive training programme tailored to meet your personal needs. This eight-week programme costs only €35.00 (one hour per week).

Swimming — Whether you're a beginner or an advanced swimmer, Westpool can offer you the best swimming in the country. We offer certification for all our courses. Starting from only €35.00.

Basketball — We offer tuition in basketball and we have the top two teams in the country. Your coach is none other than Dill Firth, the legendary basketball champion. Courses cost from €45.00 for 8 weeks.

Call Eithne on (07) 223224 for details.

1. Save this flyer as LEISURE.
2. Insert the following sentence before the last line: All our customers can avail of the sauna and Jacuzzi facilities.
3. Print one copy.

Project 17

An estate agent uses IT in a variety of ways. For example, she uses a database to track properties for sale; she uses spreadsheets to calculate the commission and to do budget analysis etc. Word processing is vital to keep vendors and buyers aware of any developments.

Time   The estimated time for this project is two hours.

Rating   This project has a difficulty rating of three.

Skills   You need the following skills to successfully complete this project:

Software Package	Tasks to Complete	Explanations (see pages)
Spreadsheet	IF, insert rows, chart	142, 140
Database	Index, find/replace	136
Word processing	Importing clip art, tabulation	122, 126

Project 17
DATABASE

Create a database for the estate agency using the following fields:

• Vendor — Name of seller
• Address — Address of house
• Beds — Number of bedrooms
• Det/Semi — Type of property, detached or semi-detached
• Negotiator — Name of salesperson
• Price — Asking price of property

'What goes up must come down. Ask any system administrator.'

Anon

FIELD NAME	WIDTH	DATATYPE
VENDOR	10	Text
ADDRESS	12	Text
BEDS	1	Numeric
DET/SEMI	9	Text
NEGOTIATOR	9	Text
PRICE	8	Currency

The database is shown below. In a real-life situation, the database would be bigger and would include property such as pubs, farms etc.

VENDOR	ADDRESS	BEDS	DET/SEMI	NEGOTIATOR	PRICE
Smith	12 East St	2	Terrace	Smith	€90,000
Bradley	23 Main St	4	Detached	Jones	€170,000
Adams	12 Main St	3	Terrace	Smith	€98,000
Jones	2 Old Rd	3	Semi	Adams	€150,000
Craig	4 New Rd	2	Terrace	Smith	€78,000
Kelly	45 Will St	3	Terrace	Adams	€124,000
Rogers	28 Gray St	3	Semi	Robinson	€89,000
Savage	1 Park St	4	Semi	Jones	€135,000
Kent	56 West St	4	Detached	Robinson	€175,000
Martin	23 East St	3	Semi	Robinson	€120,000

1 Create an index using a suitable field.
2. A customer phones to inquire about buying a three-bedroom house for under €130,000. List the houses available.
3. Another customer inquires about terraced houses. List the terraced houses available.
4. The negotiator Jones has left the agency and has been replaced by Bradley. Make the necessary changes.
5. Insert a new field called DESCRIPTION and write a short description of each house.
6. Insert the following two records:

Clarke	6 West St	4	Detached	Robinson	€155,000
Smith	3 East St	3	Semi	Bradley	€112,000

7. Print only the BEDS, DET/SEMI, PRICE and DESCRIPTION fields.
8. Search for houses in East St and print all the fields except the VENDOR field.
9. Save the database as ESTATE.

Project 17
SPREADSHEET

The estate agency uses a spreadsheet to calculate the commissions it receives and the bonus due to each negotiator. Create the following spreadsheet:

	A	B	C	D	E
1	Commission	2%			
2		Smith	Adams	Robinson	Bradley
3	Week 1	€340,000	€320,000	€220,000	€290,000
4	Week 2	€150,000	€175,000	€155,000	€20,000
5	Week 3	€279,000	€280,000	€290,000	€235,000
6	Week 4	€258,000	€190,000	€18,000	€19,500
7					
8	Total				
9	Commission				
10	Bonus				

1. In cell B8, insert a function to calculate the total sum for four weeks for Smith.
2. Copy this function to the cells in the other columns.
3. In cell B9, insert a formula to calculate the commission that Smith earned for the agency.
4. Copy this formula to the cells in the other columns.
5. In cell B10, insert a formula using the IF function to calculate whether a bonus is due or not. Negotiators get a bonus if the commission they earn is €15,000 or more. If they qualify for a bonus, they get €250; otherwise, they do not receive any further payment.
6. Insert a blank row between rows two and three, and between the rows called *Total* and *Commission*.
7. Enhance the spreadsheet as you see fit.
8. Create a chart comparing each negotiator and print a copy of the spreadsheet and the chart.
9. Save the file as ESTATE.

The estate agency wants to include a logo on its stationery. Create the following logo using a painting programme and insert it into the letter:

A1 Home Finders

Dear Ms Johnson,

Thank you for your recent telephone call inquiring about houses in your area. We currently have the following houses for sale:

Address	Bedrooms	Type	Negotiator	Price
12 East St	2	Terrace	Smith	€90,000
23 Main St	4	Det.	Jones	€170,000
12 Main St	3	Terrace	Smith	€98,000
2 Old Rd	3	Semi	Adams	€150,000

We have had an offer on 12 East St in the late eighties and we are anxious to close this sale as soon as possible.

Should you wish to view these properties you can either contact the negotiator in charge of the sale, or call to the address between 3.00 p.m. and 5.00 p.m. on Saturday.

Sincerely,

1. Set a left margin of 1 inch and a right margin of 1.5 inches.
2. Set tabs at 2 inches, 3 inches, 3.7 inches and 5.2 inches.
3. Enhance the letter as follows: make all the headings (Address, Bedrooms etc.) bold. Choose a font that is different from the rest of the document.
4. The house on 12 Main Street has been withdrawn from the market. Make the necessary changes.
5. Sign the letter with your own name and print one copy.
6. Save the letter as ESTATE.

Project 18

A building contractor uses IT applications as follows:

- Databases to track ongoing projects
- Spreadsheets to calculate salaries for his employees
- Word processing to write to clients and lawyers and to create advertisements in the press

Time   The estimated time for this project is two hours.

Rating   This project has a difficulty rating of three.

Skills   You need the following skills to successfully complete this project:

Software Package	Tasks to Complete	Explanations (see pages)
Spreadsheet	Absolute cell address	141
Database	Index, find/replace	136
Word processing	Importing clip art	122

Project 18
DATABASE

Create a database for the building contractor using the following information:

FIELD	WIDTH	DATATYPE
PURCHASER	10	Text
HOUSE	1	Text
DEPOSIT	6	Currency
PAID	1	Logical
CONTRACT	8	Date

Create a data entry form like the following:

Humpty Builders Ltd.			
Project	_____	House	_____
Deposit	_____	Paid	_____
Contract	_____		

The following database lists ten houses that the builder has sold so far in a development. Insert the following records:

PURCHASER	HOUSE	DEPOSIT	PAID	CONTRACT
Smith	E	€3,000	Y	23/4
Bradley	D	€4,000	Y	12/5
Adams	A	€4,500	N	14/6
Jones	C	€5,000	Y	12/6
Craig	A	€4,500	Y	18/7
Kelly	B	€3,000	N	7/11
Rogers	B	€3,000	Y	13/6
Savage	C	€5,000	Y	16/3
Kent	C	€5,000	N	5/12
Martin	D	€4,000	Y	8/9

1. Create an index using a suitable field.
2. List any customers who have yet to pay a deposit on their house.
3. Modifications have been made to the deposits for type C houses; the deposit is now €5,300. Search for type C houses and make the new amendments.
4. The builder has more customers who want to buy his houses. He decides to remove any customers from the current database who have not yet paid their deposit. Insert the following records in their place:

Saunders	C	€5,300	Y	23/3
French	B	€3,000	Y	5/12
Meldrew	A	€4,500	Y	8/9

5. Print the complete database and save it as BUILDER.

Project 18
SPREADSHEET

The builder uses spreadsheets to calculate the pay due to his workers. This spreadsheet uses absolute cell addresses to determine the hourly rate that an employee is paid. Create the following spreadsheet:

	A	B	C	D	E
1	Humpty Builders Ltd.				
2	Week 1			Job	Rate/Hr
3				Labourer	€10.00
4				Carpenter	€15.45
5				Plumber	€14.35
6				Plasterer	€16.45
7				Electrician	€15.35
8	Name	Job	Hours	Net	
9	Jones	Labourer	40		
10	Peters	Plasterer	40		
11	Lee	Labourer	40		
12	Menton	Carpenter	15		
13	Mitchell	Plasterer	24		
14	Firth	Carpenter	20		
15	Johnson	Plumber	35		
16	Smyth	Electrician	40		
17					

1. In cell D9, insert a formula to determine the net pay for Jones using an absolute cell address.
2. Insert the appropriate formulas for the other workers.
3. A mistake was made in the hourly rate for carpenters; it should be €16.45 and not €15.45. Correct this error.
4. A mistake was also made for employee Firth. She is an electrician. Correct this error.
5. Print one copy of the spreadsheet and save it as BUILDER.

The builder wants to create an advertisement to promote the next phase of the estate. He has drafted an idea of what he wants. Turn his idea into reality!

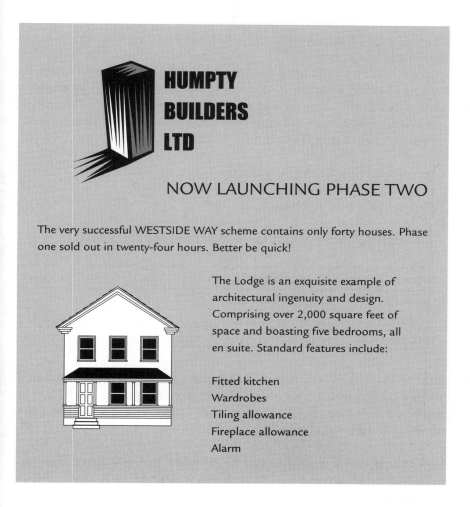

HUMPTY BUILDERS LTD

NOW LAUNCHING PHASE TWO

The very successful WESTSIDE WAY scheme contains only forty houses. Phase one sold out in twenty-four hours. Better be quick!

The Lodge is an exquisite example of architectural ingenuity and design. Comprising over 2,000 square feet of space and boasting five bedrooms, all en suite. Standard features include:

Fitted kitchen
Wardrobes
Tiling allowance
Fireplace allowance
Alarm

1. Create the advertisement. The clip art in this example was imported. However, you can create your own clip art and use it instead. Feel free to use your own words and design if you wish.
2. Print one copy of the finished advertisement and save it as BUILDER.

Project 19

The media use a variety of IT applications in their everyday work. For example, writing articles using a word processor, using databases to research topics and using spreadsheets to calculate expenses etc. In this project, you write an article for a magazine using the word processor, use a database to research an article and finally use a spreadsheet to calculate your expenses incurred as part of your research.

Time   The estimated time for this project is two hours.

Rating   This project has a difficulty rating of four.

Skills   You need the following skills to successfully complete this project:

Software Package	Tasks to Complete	Explanations (see pages)
Spreadsheet	Absolute cell address	Page 141
Database	Copy, index, query	Page 136, 134
Word processing	Find/Replace, importing clip art	Page 129, 122

Project 19
DATABASE

Most researchers used to browse newspaper clippings to find information about a story that they were researching. In fact, it was the responsibility of one person (normally the librarian or archivist) to store and sort articles and file them for later use.

For example, if you want to search for 'murders' in your county, then you would ask the librarian to collect the clippings pertinent to murder and your county. You could then browse the information. This could take some time. Naturally, a computer is much more suited for this purpose. Most newspapers and magazines are now automating these searches using databases. There are a number of advantages: the speed of response and multiple users can access the information at the same time.

Retrieve the database file MAGAZINE from the Web site. There are only ten records (corresponding to the ten articles listed) in this database. Normally another field showing the contents of the article would be present, but it is not included in this database.

AUTHOR	DATE	KEYWORDS	LOCATION
Smith	23/4/99	Robbery, violence	A
Smith	12/5/87	Murder, terrorism, violence	A
Craig	14/6/98	Fraud, banks, finance	B
Smith	12/6/00	Murder, extradition, violence	A
Craig	18/7/99	Tribunal, fraud	B
Kelly	7/11/99	Shares, flotation, finance	B
Kelly	13/6/99	House prices, finance	B
Martin	16/3/98	Clothes, fashion, model	C
Smith	5/12/97	Extradition, terrorism, violence	A
Martin	8/9/89	Fashion, model, money	C

1. Copy the database to your own drive and save it as MAG.
2. Create an index using a suitable field.
3. As part of your research, you are browsing for articles about murder. List the relevant articles.
4. You know that the author Smith normally writes about violence. List all the articles that Smith wrote since 1 January 1999.
5. Another journalist is writing an article about money laundering (a fraud offence). Search for any articles that might be of interest.
6. Print the AUTHOR, DATE and KEYWORDS fields only.
7. Enhance the database as you see fit and save it.

Project 19
SPREADSHEET

Each journalist must submit an expense sheet at the end of each month to claim expenses. The journalists use a spreadsheet to calculate how much they are entitled to. Create the following spreadsheet, and then carry out the instructions:

	A	B	C	D	E
1	Jan			Allowances	
2				Mileage	€0.75
3				Lunch	€5.00
4				Overnight	€60.00
5					
6	Allowance	Smith	Craig	Kelly	Martin
7	Miles Travelled	50	45	68	34
8	Net				
9	Lunches	5	2	7	9
10	Net				
11	Overnights	2	0	2	7
12	Net				
13	Train/Bus	0	0	€12.30	€13.50
14	Net				
15	Total				

1. Insert a formula in cell B8 to calculate the mileage allowance applicable for Smith (use an absolute cell address).
2. Copy this formula to the cells in the other columns.
3. Insert in cell B10 a formula to calculate the lunch allowance for Smith using the absolute cell address system as before. Copy this formula to the cells in the other columns.
4. Insert a formula in cell B12, using the absolute cell address to calculate the overnight allowance for Smith. Copy the formula to the cells in the other columns.
5. In cell B14, insert the value of B13 (i.e. the train or bus fare). Copy the formula to the cells in the other columns.
6. In cell B15, insert a formula to add the contents of cells B8, B10, B12 and B14. Copy the formula to the cells in the other columns.
7. Enhance it as you see fit. Print one copy and save the file as MAG.

As a journalist working on the magazine, you are asked to submit an article on fashion and to include a graphic. The article below is an example of what is required, but feel free to make up your own!

FASHION HOUSES ANNOUNCE NEW LINES FOR AUTUMN

By
Your Name

Leading fashion houses yesterday unveiled their new lines for autumn. All the leading houses were represented in the Italian home of fashion, Milan.

NEW COLOURS
New colours for this autumn are baby blue, cerise pink, gold, ice white and mellow yellow (not necessarily on the same garment). This marks a departure from the normally dull 'autumnal' colours that usually pervade the fashion scene at this time of year.

NEW SHAPES
As with colours, new shapes have made a debut this year. Chief among the designs are long-flowing dresses, short-sleeved blouses and a marked absence of hats!

1. Create the article. Feel free to insert your own comments about fashion! The clip art in this example was imported. However, you can insert your own clip art and use it instead.
2. Use the Find/Replace facility to replace the word *fashion* with *haute couture*.
3. Enhance the article as you see fit.
4. Print one copy of the finished article and save it as MAGAZINE.

Project 20

This project explores how a livestock mart could use IT. The word processing part of this assignment creates invoices for a sale. The database shows how marts keep track of the animals they are selling. The spreadsheet is an example of an invoice that the mart produces for each farmer.

Time   The estimated time for this project is two hours.

Rating   This project has a difficulty rating of four.

Skills   You need the following skills to successfully complete this project:

Software Package	Tasks to Complete	Explanations (see pages)
Spreadsheet	Absolute cell address	141
Database	Copy, index, query	136, 134
Word processing	Copy from a spreadsheet	122

Project 20

DATABASE

It is vital that a mart can track the animals it sells, because of the risk of TB, BSE etc. These diseases can enter the human food chain, so the mart must be able to track the medical records of all the cattle it sells for slaughter. All animals are tagged with a number, and have a card that shows when they were last tested. The database contains the following information:

FIELD	WIDTH	DATATYPE
NAME	10	Text
DATE	8	Date
BREED	10	Text
PRICE	6	Currency
TAG	6	Alphanumeric
TESTED	8	Text
WEIGHT	3	Numeric

Retrieve the file MART from the Web site. There are only ten records (corresponding to ten animals) in this database:

NAME	DATE	BREED	PRICE	TAG	TESTED	WEIGHT
Smith	12/4/00	Hereford	€560	YHR13346	13/2/00	620
Bradley	14/5/00	Limousin	€640	FRG66455	16/4/00	380
Adams	24/3/00	Hereford	€490	YHR75428	12/1/00	580
Jones	27/6/00	Charolais	€720	YHR25622	15/5/00	650
Craig	13/3/00	Hereford	€590	YHR66363	4/12/99	640
Kelly	14/4/00	Charolais	€690	YHR67883	13/12/99	630
Rogers	23/4/00	Limousin	€610	FRG33213	2/1/00	390
Savage	29/8/00	Charolais	€710	YHR4247	21/8/00	640
Kent	16/7/00	Hereford	€580	YHR42266	9/4/00	635
Martin	25/6/00	Hereford	€530	YHR25255	25/4/00	595

1. Copy the database to your own drive and save it under the name MART.
2. Create an index using a suitable field.
3. Insert the following two records:

Smith	6/7/00	Hereford	€580	YHR45266	19/4/00	645
Your Name	15/6/00	Hereford	€530	YHR28255	15/4/00	600

4. Search for cattle tested before 1 February 2000 and print the results.
5. Search for Hereford cattle and print the following fields: NAME, BREED, PRICE and TESTED.
6. Enhance the database as you see fit.
7. Save the database as MART1 and print it.

When farmers buy animals at a mart, they are given an invoice at the end of trading showing how many cattle they sold or bought, and how much they owe or are owed.

	A	B	C	D	E
1	Livestock	Mart			
2		Commission	2%		
3	Name	Your Name			
4	Bought				
5	Lot No.	Description	Number	Weight	Price
6	12	Dry Cattle	2	1,240	€1,105
7	32	Lambs	11	534	€430
8	45	Lambs	13	560	€512
9	Total				
10	Sold				
11	Lot No.	Description	Number	Weight	Price
12	8	Dry Cattle	1	640	€590
13	54	Ewes	7	420	€145
14	Total				
15	Commission				

1. Create the above spreadsheet.
2. Insert in cell F5 the title *Price/Kg.*
3. Insert a formula in cell F6 to calculate the price per kilogram and copy this formula to the other cells in the column.
4. Insert a formula in cell C9 to calculate the total number of animals bought. Copy this formula across to the other cells in the row.
5. Insert in cell C14 a similar formula to calculate the total number of animals sold. Copy this formula to the other cells in the row.
6. Insert a formula in cell B15 to calculate the commission due to the mart. (This will be 2% of the price of the total sold plus 2% of the price of the total bought.) Use an absolute cell address for this.
7. Enhance the spreadsheet as you see fit.
8. Save the database as MART and print one copy.

The mart creates an invoice for each farmer using both word processing and spreadsheets. For this example, you must import (copy/paste) the relevant information from the spreadsheet.

LIVESTOCK MART

To:	Your Name
Date:	Today's Date
Re:	Sale/Purchase of Animals

The following lots were sold/purchased on your behalf today:

Commission 2%

Name	Your Name

Bought

Lot No.	Description	Number	Weight	Price
12	Dry Cattle	2	1,240	€1,105
32	Lambs	11	534	€430
45	Lambs	13	560	€512

Total

Sold

Lot No.	Description	Number	Weight	Price
8	Dry Cattle	1	640	€590
54	Ewes	7	420	€145

Total

Commission

Please forward payment by 12 March 2000.

'The computer programmer is a creator of universes for which he alone is responsible. Universes of virtually unlimited complexity can be created in the form of computer programmes.'

Joseph Weizenbaum

1. Create the previous letter.
2. Insert the information from the spreadsheet using copy/paste.
3. Insert your name and today's date.
4. Enhance the letter as appropriate.
5. Print one copy of the document.
6. Save the letter as MART.

Project 21

In this project, you see how a Montessori school uses IT to manage its business. In the word processing section, you create a flyer using columns. You use the database to create labels for the flyers, and you use spreadsheets to calculate the weekly income.

Time The estimated time for this project is two hours.

Rating This project has a rating of four.

Skills You need the following skills to successfully complete this project:

Software Package	Tasks to Complete	Explanations (see pages)
Spreadsheet	Absolute cell address	141
Database	Copy, index, labels	136, 137
Word processing	Columns, clip art	128

Project 21
DATABASE

The Montessori school keeps a record of parent details on the database. It uses this information to generate labels with the name and address of each parent. In this way, a standard letter can be sent to each parent, and the label can be used to address the envelope. This saves a lot of time addressing envelopes manually. The database has the following structure:

FIELD	WIDTH	DATATYPE
TITLE	3	Text
FIRSTNAME	10	Text
SURNAME	12	Text
ADDRESS1	20	Text
ADDRESS2	12	Text
CHILD	10	Text

Retrieve the file MONT from the Web site. The database contains the following ten records:

TITLE	FIRSTNAME	SURNAME	ADDRESS1	ADDRESS2	CHILD
Ms	Ita	McCafferty	2 East Park	Westpool	Callum
Mr	Dill	Jones	23 Main St	Westpool	Simon
Dr	Garrett	Campbell	45 Dale Road	Jamestown	Gweneth
Mrs	Dymphna	O' Looney	34 Main St	Jamestown	James
Ms	Martina	Firth	12 Pearse Rd	Westpool	Anna
Mrs	Jane	Ferry	34 Coronation St	Westpool	Hilda
Mr	James	Johnson	76 Martin Tce	Westpool	Donal
Mrs	Caroline	Connell	211 Westwood Park	Jamestown	James
Ms	Lucy	Kent	87 Main St	Jamestown	Darragh
Ms	Hilda	West	3 Main St	Westpool	Luca

1. Copy the database to your own drive. Save it under the name MONT. Enhance it as appropriate.
2. Create an index using a suitable field.
3. Insert the following two records into the correct positions:

Ms	Noreen	Kavandish	12 Long Road	Westpool	Regina
Mr	William	Stewart	32 The Rise	Jamestown	Nigel

4. Search for anyone living in Main St in Jamestown. The flyers will be delivered by hand to these addresses.
5. Create labels, which can fit two-across an A4 page, as follows.
   <TITLE> <FIRSTNAME> <SURNAME>
   <ADDRESS1>
   <ADDRESS2>
6. Print the labels and a copy of the complete database.

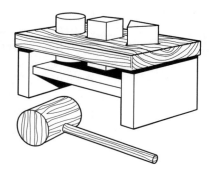

The Montessori school uses a spreadsheet to calculate the number of times a child uses the school during a week. The spreadsheet is set up as a template, which can be used again. Create the following spreadsheet:

	A	B	C	D	E
1	KIDS SKOOL				
2		Half-Day	€9.00		
3		Full-Day	€18.00		
4					
5	First Name	Surname	Half	Full	Total
6	Callum	McCafferty	2	3	
7	Simon	Jones	0	5	
8	Gweneth	Campbell	1	4	
9	James	O'Looney	0	5	
10	Anna	Firth	3	2	
11	Hilda	Ferry	0	5	
12	Donal	Johnson	3	2	
13	James	Connell	0	5	
14	Darragh	Kent	4	1	
15	Luca	West	1	4	

1. Insert a formula in E6, using absolute cell addresses, to calculate the total cost of half-days and full-days for Callum Mc Cafferty.
2. Copy this formula to the other rows.
3. Format column E as currency values, which are accurate to two decimal places.
4. Insert the word *Total* in A17. Insert a formula in cell C17 to calculate the total cost of fees for half-days during the week. (Use an absolute cell address.) Insert a similar formula in D17 to calculate the total cost of fees for full-days for the week. Insert a formula to add these two values in E17.
5. Insert the word *Percentage* in A18. In cell E18, insert a formula to calculate the half-day fees (C17) as a percentage of the total.
6. Create a chart (stacked column is best) to compare the half-days with the full-days. Print the chart and spreadsheet.

The school sends regular flyers to parents to keep them updated about current events. It posts these flyers using the labels created in the database to address the envelopes.

Welcome to our regular newsletter. For those of you who have just sent your child to KIDS SKOOL, we extend a warm welcome. A meeting was held on Wednesday night last to chart the progress of the school to date. The meeting was very well attended, almost 100% attendance. A number of items were raised. Some of the more important points were as follows:

1. School fees
2. Collection of infants from school
3. Medical care

In summary, the school fees were raised last month by 5%. This was due to circumstances beyond our control. Infants are to be collected only by the persons designated on the registration card. This is an absolute requirement.

Some parents were worried that their children could contract diseases from other children e.g. mumps etc. A doctor is on call at all times and can be at the centre within 10 - 15 minutes. A nurse attends the school at all times. All our staff have first aid qualifications. If your child is unwell, he or she should be treated first by the family doctor.

1. Create the flyer and insert clip art as appropriate.
2. Type the text without columns. When you are satisfied with the text, change the layout to columns. You may decide to use a different number of columns from the example.
3. Enhance as appropriate. Save the flyer as MONT and print one copy.

Project 22

In this project, a garden centre uses IT to successfully run its business. It uses the following applications:

- Word processing to create flyers for door-to-door delivery
- Database to catalogue its stock of plants
- Spreadsheets to calculate wages and bonuses

Time The estimated time for this project is two hours.

Rating This project has a rating of four.

Skills You need the following skills to successfully complete this project:

Software Package	Tasks to Complete	Explanations (see pages)
Spreadsheet	Absolute cell address, IF with AND, copy	141, 143
Database	Design, create, input	131, 134
Word processing	Columns, clip art	128

Project 22
DATABASE

The garden centre has decided to create a database of its existing stock of plants. It has a list of plants showing the name, when it flowers, whether it has a scent etc. You must design and create a database to hold this information. Plan the database on paper before creating the fields etc. Plan for the following:

- FIELD NAME
- FIELD WIDTH
- FIELD DATATYPE

Is any information irrelevant? Remember the database is initially for the employees of the garden centre to answer customer queries efficiently. Later, the database might become part of a multimedia development, and customers may want to ask their own questions.

Bearing all this in mind, design and create the database, using the following information:

- **Delphinium elatum**, likes sunny, well-drained sites. It flowers from June to July showing white, cream and blue shades. It can grow up to eight feet, needs support.
- **Purple cornflower** can grow up to four feet, it has a strong scent and likes sunny, well-drained sites. It is undemanding.
- **Honeysuckle** can grow up to twenty feet and has a beautiful scent. The colours vary from red to yellow. It likes shady, well-drained sites. Flowering times vary.
- **Rhododendrons** need an acid soil, like shady well-drained sites. They flower in every colour except blue! Flowering times vary from February to August. They can reach twenty feet in height.
- **Primroses** flower from March to July and can grow up to three feet. They have a variety of colours and need a shady well-drained site with humus-rich soil. Most have a scent.

- **Lavender** flowers from July to Spetember and can grow up to four feet. Has an aromatic scent and shows white, blue or purple flowers. Needs a sunny, dry site.
- **Mint** needs a sunny dry site and has a wonderful minty scent. It flowers between August and October and can grow up to six feet. It needs a sunny, dry site with rich soil.
- **Meadowsweet** flowers in the middle of summer and prefers a shady, damp aspect. It can grow up to five feet and shows white, pink or yellow flowers.

- **Snowdrop** can grow up to ten inches and flowers appear from January to March. The flowers are white. It prefers a shady, damp environment.
- **Bluebell** flowers from April to June. It can have pink or white flowers, as well as the familiar blue. Bluebells can grow up to sixteen inches and like a damp, shady site.

1. Create an index using a suitable field.
2. A customer asks for information about plants that like shady habitats. What plants are suitable?
3. Another customer asks for information about scented plants. She insists that the plants must tolerate shade. What plants fulfil her criteria?
4. A customer asks about plants that flower in January. Are there any?
5. Which plants need a sunny site?
6. Print one copy of the database, and save it as GARDEN.

Project 22
SPREADSHEET

The garden centre uses spreadsheets in the day-to-day running of its business. It uses the spreadsheet to calculate the bonuses of the employees. Retrieve the file GARDEN from the Web site. It contains the following information:

	A	B	C	D	E
1					
2	Name	Smith	Jones	Willis	Ford
3	Hrs/Week1	48	48	42	40
4	Hrs/Week2	40	45	45	40
5	Hrs/Week3	45	50	50	40
6	Hrs/Week4	50	55	55	50
7					
8	Rate/Hr	€6.75			
9	OvrTime	€12.00			
10	Bonus	€50.00			
11					
12	Sales 1				
13	Sales 2				
14	Sales 3				
15	Sales 4				
16					
17	Total Hrs				
18	Total Sales				
19	Bonus				

1. Open the spreadsheet GARDEN.
2. Also open the spreadsheet GSALES that contains the sales each employee made during this four-week period. Copy this information and insert it into cells B12 to E15. Link the copied cells to the SALES spreadsheet, in case they are updated.
3. In cell B17, insert a formula to calculate the total hours worked by Smith. Copy the formula across to the cells for each employee.
4. In cell B18, insert a formula to calculate the total sales for Smith. Copy this formula across to the cells for each employee.
5. In cell B19, insert a formula to calculate the bonus, if any, each worker should get. A worker gets a bonus if the total number of hours worked, in a four-week period, is greater than 180, and the total sales is greater than €400. If the worker qualifes for a bonus, then insert €50, otherwise €0.
6. Print one copy of the spreadsheet.
7. Change the sales figures in the file GSALES to see if they automatically update in GARDEN.

A garden centre wants to create a flyer for door-to-door delivery to increase business and to advertise its spring sale. Create the following flyer, using clip art where necessary to add impact to your message. Feel free to use your own text.

Welcome to Green Finger Garden Centre News!

Our garden centre is totally devoted to Organic Gardening. You won't find a man-made chemical in our centre.

In response to customer demand, we now stock **Organic Fertiliser** (made from poultry manure). The roses will love this.

It is also suitable for new lawns to give them a good initial growth.

Organic Fruit Plants
As usual, we have a wide range of organic plants and fruit trees that have never been exposed to artificial fertilisers or sprays. Your blackcurrant jam will taste fabulous with the berries from our new range of blackcurrant bushes.

Garden Accessories
We stock a wide range of garden accessories e.g. lawn mowers, shears, pruning knives, gloves, wheelbarrows, barbecues, spades, forks, seats and furniture etc. If we don't stock an item you require, please tell us and we'll order any item you want.

1. Create the flyer, use clip art to enhance it.
2. Create columns (you may use fewer columns, if necessary).
3. Enhance the heading.
4. Save the file as GARDEN, and print one copy.

Project 23

An electrical power supply company uses IT in many ways. It uses a database to track customer details e.g. last bill, number of units used etc. It uses spreadsheets to calculate the payment due from each customer. It also uses word processing to send bills to customers, order supplies, deal with complaints etc.

Time   The estimated time for this project is two hours.

Rating   This project has a rating of four.

Skills   You need the following skills to successfully complete this project:

Software Package	Tasks to Complete	Explanations (see pages)
Spreadsheet	Absolute cell address	141
Database	Index, labels	136, 137
Word processing	Form fields, copy	129, 122

Project 23

DATABASE

The power company uses a database to track customer details. The database has the following structure:

FIELD NAME	WIDTH	DATATYPE	DESCRIPTION
NAME	12	Text	Name of customer
ADDRESS1	18	Text	First line of customer address
ADDRESS2	15	Text	Second line of customer address
ACCOUNT	9	Numeric	Account number
BILL	7	Currency	Bill amount
DATE	8	Date	Date of issue

'The most overlooked advantage to owning a computer is that if they foul up, there's no law against whacking them around a little.'

Peter Porterfield

Retrieve the file POWER. The database contains the following information:

NAME	ADDRESS1	ADDRESS2	ACCOUNT	BILL	DATE
J Smith	1 Main St	Westpool	223244456	€45.56	12/4/00
I Williams	2 Market Sq	Milford	224677889	€76.89	13/4/00
K Lucy	15 Woodstown Dale	Knocklyon	664443362	€34.65	14/4/00
P Burke	44 Canny Pk	Sligo	556732217	€89.54	14/4/00
J Martin	23 Abbey St	Jamestown	242477224	€123.74	12/4/00
A Grier	178 James Tce	Williamstown	166427767	€56.43	12/4/00
A Sweeney	43 Westpark Way	Milford	356334567	€78.65	29/3/00
S Kerr	18 New Park	Jamestown	241678124	€84.64	24/3/00
T Nelson	34 West Mall	Westpool	488675933	€93.35	28/3/00
N Conlon	45 East Mall	Westpool	266533743	€74.79	13/4/00

1. Insert a new column called ADDRESS3. Enter the following information: Kildare, Donegal, Dublin, Sligo, Tipperary, Clare, Donegal, Tipperary, Kildare and Kildare.
2. Create an index using a suitable field.
3. A bill is considered overdue if it has not been paid within fifteen days of issue. Today's date is 15 April 2000. Search for all overdue bills.
4. Create a label format similar to the following:
   <NAME>
   <ADDRESS1>
   <ADDRESS2>
   <ADDRESS3>
5. Using this label format, print labels for all customers whose bills are overdue.
6. Insert a formula to add the contents of the BILL field.
7. Save the file as POWER. Print a copy of the complete database.

The power supply company uses a spreadsheet to calculate the amount owed by each customer. The spreadsheet contains the following information:

	A	B	C	D	E
1	Name				
2	Account	3651 33 444	Rates		
3			Day	€0.0745	
4			Night	€0.0534	
5	Readings				
6	Present	Previous	Units	Description	Amount
7	972	591	381	General Domestic	
8			100	Night Charge	
9					
10		VAT a 12.5% on			
11		Round			
12					
13	Usage Period	Reading Date		Payment Date	Total
14	Feb-Mar 00	28 April 00		13 May 00	

1. Create the spreadsheet.
2. Insert a formula in cell E7 to calculate the general domestic charge (i.e. day rate) using an absolute cell address.
3. Insert a similar formula in cell E8 to calculate the night charge, again using the absolute cell address system.
4. In cell C10, insert a function to add the contents of E7 and E8.
5. In cell E10, insert a formula to calculate VAT on the value in C10.
6. In cell E11, insert a function to round this amount to the nearest euro. Insert the amount in E14.
7. Enhance the spreadsheet as appropriate. Print one copy of the complete spreadsheet.
8. Save the file as POWER.

Set up the following standard letter as a template, which you can use again:

POWER ENERGY
Power House
Kinsale

Date

Dear <NAME>,

Your last bill for <AMOUNT> was sent to you on <DATE> and still has not been paid.

This account is now overdue. Failure to pay within the next seven days will unfortunately result in disconnection. Reconnection may take some time and will incorporate a reconnection fee of €60.00.

We accept partial repayments over a number of months in some circumstances. If you wish to avail of this, contact Brenda on 0800 112 113.

I enclose your last bill amount below.

1. Create the letter and insert the form fields: NAME, AMOUNT and DATE.
2. Insert a copy of the bill, created in the spreadsheet section of this project, after the last line.
3. Sign the letter.
4. Enhance the letter as appropriate.
5. Save it as POWER.
6. Protect the document from changes by assigning a password. (Note: the form fields must still accept input.)
7. Insert today's date and use your own name for the NAME field. Insert €65.00 in the AMOUNT field. Choose a date from two months ago for the DATE field.
8. Print a copy of the letter.

Project 24

A telephone company uses IT in many areas of its business as follows:

- Different databases to track customer details e.g. last bill, number of calls, type of call etc
- Spreadsheets to calculate the payment due for each customer
- Word processing to send bills to customers, order supplies, deal with complaints etc.

Time   The estimated time for this project is two hours.

Rating   This project has a rating of four.

Skills   You need the following skills to successfully complete this project:

Software Package	Tasks to Complete	Explanations (see pages)
Spreadsheet	Absolute cell address, linking spreadsheets	141
Database	Index, labels	136, 137
Word processing	Linking with a spreadsheet	122

Project 24
DATABASE

The telephone company uses a number of databases to track customer details. This is an example of one database. It has the following structure:

FIELD NAME	WIDTH	DATATYPE	DESCRIPTION
NAME	15	Text	Name of customer
ADDRESS1	18	Text	First line of customer address
ADDRESS2	15	Text	Second line of customer address
ACCOUNT	10	Numeric	Account number
TELEPHONE	10	Numeric	Telephone number
DATE	8	Date	Date of bill issue
AMOUNT	7	Currency	Amount due

Retrieve the file PHONE from the Web site. The database contains the following information:

NAME	ADDRESS1	ADDRESS2	ACCOUNT	TEL	DATE	AMOUNT
M Summers	1 Main St	Westpool	235 4456	01 555322	22/5/00	€130.34
L Brinkly	2 Market Sq	Milford	675 7889	02 884332	17/5/00	€90.87
R Roberts	1 Parkway	Jamestown	664 6842	03 334224	4/5/00	€67.84
A McBeal	4 Lunny Pk	Sligo	221 5834	07 993335	20/5/00	€68.89
J McEnroe	3 Abbey Tce	Jamestown	345 9143	03 554332	22/5/00	€93.45
S Sunny	8 James Tce	Williamstown	784 3211	08 548898	2/5/00	€95.78
M Claire	43 St Catherine's	Milford	331 3632	02 426788	29/4/00	€140.45
D Kelly	58 New Park	Jamestown	342 0435	03 647223	14/4/00	€120.23
P Burke	34 West Pk	Westpool	234 5164	01 663727	18/5/00	€56.73
J Ferry	10 St Catherine's	Westpool	466 5634	01 113464	13/5/00	€45.65

1. Insert a new field called PAID. Enter the following information:
   Yes, Yes, No, Yes, No, No, Yes, Yes, No, Yes.
2. Create an index using a suitable field.
3. A mistake was made in the bill amount for R Roberts. It should read €87.64. Correct this error.
4. Search for customers whose bills are unpaid. Save this query as UNPAID.
5. A bill is overdue if it is unpaid after fifteen days. Today's date is 22 May 2000. Search the UNPAID file for any bills that are overdue.
6. Create a label with the following format:
   <NAME>
   <ADDRESS1>
   <ADDRESS2>
7. Using this label format, print labels for all customers whose bills are unpaid.
8. Save the file as PHONE and print a copy of the database.

The phone company uses spreadsheets to calculate the bill payment for each customer. The main spreadsheet looks like the following:

	A	B	C	D
1	NAME			
2	ACCOUNT	365 2344		
3	TEL NO	01 4953054		
4	TYPE	RESIDENCE		
5	Rental From	19/10/00	To	18/12/00
6	Calls From	09/09/00	To	16/10/00
7				
8	Line Rental			€24.50
9	Equipment Rental			€2.40
10	Calls	Units	Rates	
11	Local (1 unit)		€0.095	
12	Local (2 - 4 units)		€0.095	
13	Local (over 4 units)		€0.115	
14	Inland		€0.225	
15	VAT ∂ 21%			

1. The values for B11 to B14 are in another spreadsheet called PHONE1. The PHONE1 spreadsheet shows the units that the customer used, and the date the call was made.
2. Open file PHONE1 and insert a function to add the total number of calls in columns B, C, D and E.
3. Copy these (Paste/Link) to cells B11, B12, B13 and B14.
4. Insert functions to calculate the amount payable in cells D11 to D14.
5. Insert a formula to calculate the VAT payable.
6. Create a pie chart showing what percentage the calls and VAT make up in the final bill. You will use the pie chart in the word processing section.
7. Finally calculate the total amount payable. Save the file as PHONE and print one copy.

Set up a standard letter, which you can use as a template.

THE TELEPHONY CO.
BELL House
CORK

Dear Name,

Thank you for your enquiry regarding your recent bill. Your bill can be divided into the following parts:

Line Rental   €24.50
Equipment Rental   €2.40

Calls
84 local (1 unit)
15 local (2 – 4 units)
7 local (over 4 units)
30 inland
VAT @ 21%

You can see from the following chart how the calls break down:

1. Create the previous letter and insert the bill data from the spreadsheet.
2. Insert the chart from the spreadsheet. (Make sure that the spreadsheet data is linked to the letter to take account of future changes.)
3. Enhance the letter as you see fit.
4. Change the following data in the spreadsheet:
   • Change the 2 – 4 local-call rate from €0.095 to €0.1
   • Change the VAT rate to 22%
   These changes must be automatically reflected in the word processing document.
5. Sign the letter and save it as PHONE. Print a copy of the letter.

Project 25

A firm of stockbrokers uses IT in all its share dealings as follows:

- A database to store all customer dealings and to track portfolios efficiently
- Word processing to send clients contract notes for shares that were bought or sold and letters to advise clients of which shares to buy or sell
- Spreadsheets to do a variety of tasks from risk analysis to charting the progress of a share

Time The estimated time for this project is two hours.

Rating This project has a rating of four.

Skills You need the following skills to successfully complete this project:

Software Package	Tasks to Complete	Explanations (see pages)
Spreadsheet	Absolute cell address, using IF	141, 142
Database	SUM	135
Word processing	Linking with a spreadsheet	122

Project 25
DATABASE

The stockbroker uses databases for a wide range of tasks. The following is an example of the type of database:

FIELD NAME	WIDTH	DATATYPE	DESCRIPTION
NAME	12	Text	Name of customer
ACCOUNT	6	Numeric	Account number
DATE	8	Date	Date of transaction
BUY/SELL	4	Text	Whether the share was bought or sold
SHARE	10	Text	Name of the share
PRICE	7	Currency	Price of the share
UNITS	4	Numeric	Number of shares bought or sold

Retrieve the file STOCK from the Web site. The database contains the following information:

NAME	ACCOUNT	DATE	BUY/SELL	SHARE	PRICE (euros)	UNITS
N Jagger	A22667	12/3/00	BUY	SMURFIT	−€2.80	4,500
M Jackson	A22753	14/2/00	SELL	AIB	€14.50	60
P Jones	F44325	23/3/00	BUY	AIB	−€14.75	70
N Jagger	A22667	1/4/00	SELL	EIRCOM	€5.10	3,400
J Howard	B43374	4/7/00	BUY	CRH	−€12.57	56
B Lynch	G83227	6/3/00	SELL	BOI	€17.80	80
A Adams	T99527	16/5/00	BUY	BOI	−€18.22	50
N Jagger	Y45772	28/4/00	BUY	SMURFIT	−€2.95	3,000
P Jones	R45727	26/5/00	SELL	KERRY	€12.90	59
B Lynch	W2727	17/7/00	BUY	CRH	−€12.50	80

1. Format the PRICE field to two decimal places.
2. Insert a new field called TOTAL. Insert a function to multiply the PRICE by the UNITS field. Format the field as currency values, which are accurate to two decimal places.
3. Insert another field called COMMISSION. Insert a formula to calculate the commission at a flat rate of 1.5%.
4. Search for all N Jagger's transactions. Insert a formula to calculate the net profit or loss (use the SUM function).
5. Enhance the database as appropriate.
6. Save the database as STOCK. Print one copy of the complete database.

The broker uses spreadsheets to calculate the commission due, which depends on the size of the transaction. Create the following spreadsheet:

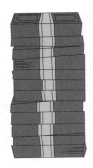

	A	B	C	D	E	F	G
1	NAME N Jagger						
2	**ACCOUNT**	A22667					
3							
4							
5							
6	Transaction	Advice	Date	Price	Units	Total	Commission
7	Buy Smurfit	Y	28/4/00	€2.95	3,000		
8	Sell Eircom	N	1/4/00	€5.10	3,400		
9	Buy Smurfit	N	12/3/00	€2.80	4,500		
10	Total						
11	Commission	Charge					
12	Up to €4,000	€20.00					
13	Over €4,000	1.5%					
14	Advice	€60.00					
15							

1. Insert a formula in cell F7 to calculate the total price. Copy this formula to the other cells for transactions.
2. Insert a formula in G7 to calculate the commission due using the IF function. Commission is at a flat rate of €20.00 if the transaction is up to €4,000. If the transaction is worth more than this, then the fee is 1.5% of the total transaction. In addition, if advice was sought, an additional fee of €60.00 is added.
3. Insert the word *Advice* in cell H6. Insert a formula in cell H7 to calculate the fee for advice using the IF function. Copy this formula to the other rows. Finally, insert the word *Total* in cell I6. Insert a formula in cell I7 to calculate the total fees due (i.e. commission and advice). Copy this formula to the other rows.
4. Insert a formula to calculate the total commission due in cell G10. Copy this formula to columns H and I.
5. Enhance the spreadsheet as you see fit. Print one copy and save it as BROKER.

Create the following letter, which will be sent to a client:

THE HONEST BROKER
Treasury House
Wall St

Today's Date

ANALYSIS OF SHARES

Despite the poor results from the last quarter, we strongly support KemiKall, which we rate as a strong **buy**. The share price has weakened considerably over the past four months going from a high of $45.56 in July to $23.44 this month. At a price to earnings ratio (P/E) of only 12.3, this share should stage a recovery in the short term.

Owners of SafeNuc should consider either taking profits (if you bought shares at the right time), or selling their holdings. The company issued a profit warning last week, which saw the price of the share fall from $16.53 to $12.22 in one day. If you bought SafeNuc recently you might consider selling at a loss. This share has been overpriced for some months now. We rate this a strong **sell**.

In the medium to long term, we rate FarmIcal, the leading pharmaceutical company specialising in the agricultural sector, a **buy**. At $11.12 and with a P/E of 14.5 this share should hold strongly over the coming year.

1. Set margins of 1.5 inches (left) and 1 inch (right).
2. Create the letter.
3. Insert a copy of the bill, created in the spreadsheet section of this project, after the last line.
4. Sign the letter with your own name.
5. Enhance the letter as appropriate.
6. Save the file as STOCK.
7. Protect the document from changes by assigning a password.
8. Print one copy of the letter.

Project 26

IT applications play a critical part in the administration of a hospital. Patient records are often stored on a database. Spreadsheets are used to invoice patients or their insurance agencies for the cost of treatment. Word processing is used in internal memos and documents as well as in correspondence with external suppliers etc.

Time   The estimated time for this project is two hours.

Rating   This project has a difficulty rating of five.

Skills   You need the following skills to successfully complete this project:

Software Package	Tasks to Complete	Explanations (see pages)
Spreadsheet	Absolute cell address, COUNTIF	141, 144
Database	Index, labels	136, 137
Word processing	Mailmerge with database	130

Project 26

DATABASE

The hospital uses a database to track patients, the date they entered hospital, their symptoms, the doctor in charge etc. The structure of the database is as follows:

FIELD NAME	WIDTH	DATATYPE	DESCRIPTION
NAME	12	Text	Patient's name
ADDRESS1	12	Text	First line of address
ADDRESS2	12	Text	Second line of address
DATE	8	Date	Date of admission
DOCTOR	10	Text	Doctor in charge
WARD	3	Text	Name of ward
SYMPTOMS	30	Text	Type of symptoms
PRIVATE	1	Logical	Is the patient private or not?

Retrieve the file HOSP from the Web site. The database contains the following information:

NAME	ADDRESS1	ADDRESS2	DATE	DOCTOR	WARD	SYMPTOMS	PRIVATE
J Martin	41 Main St	Westpool	12/3/00	Kent	A	Nausea, sore ear	Y
A Grier	4 Market Sq	Milford	13/4/00	Clarke	C	Sore throat	Y
S Kerr	10 Parkway	Jamestown	11/3/00	Kent	A	Temperature, nausea	N
V Cloon	12 New Rd	Sligo	1/4/00	Clarke	B	Broken leg	Y
N Daly	3 Abbey Tce	Jamestown	23/3/00	Kent	ICU	Chest pains	N
N Conlon	8 James Tce	Jamestown	15/4/00	Kent	A	Broken arm	Y
P Rooney	43 New Rd	Milford	7/3/00	Molloy	ICU	Pain in left arm	N
T Nelson	58 New Park	Jamestown	3/2/00	Doherty	B	Temperature, rash	N
P Burke	34 West Pk	Westpool	4/3/00	Robinson	C	Swollen eye	Y
K Clarke	10 St James	Westpool	4/4/00	Doherty	ICU	Dizziness, nausea	Y

1. Create an index using the DATE field as the primary key.
2. Enhance it as you see fit and insert these records:

J Gold	12 New Rd	Milford	5/4/00	Kent	ICU	Chest pains	Y
I Silke	13 West Tce	Westpool	12/4/00	Robinson	C	Sore throat, nausea	Y

3. Search for patients in the intensive care unit (ICU).
4. Dr Kent is on holiday and her replacement is Dr Markson. Make this change.
5. Search for patients admitted in March 2000. Print only the NAME, ADDRESS1, ADDRESS2 and SYMPTOMS fields for this search.
6. Search for patients who do not have private health insurance and create labels for them.
7. Search for patients suffering from nausea. Print the results of this search.
8. Save the file as HOSP and print one copy of the complete database.

The hospital uses spreadsheets to determine when a bed will become available in a two-week period:

	A	B	C	D	E	F	G	H
1	BED							
2	Period	1/3/00						
3								
4		1	2	3	4	5	6	7
5	Ward							
6	A							
7	B							
8	C							
9	ICU							
10	Availability							
11	A							
12	B							
13	C							
14	ICU							
15								

1. Create the previous spreadsheet.
2. Retrieve the spreadsheet HOSP from the Web site and open it. This spreadsheet lists the expected length of stay of each patient in the seven beds in each ward. Copy this information to the block of cells B6 to H9.
3. Insert a formula in B11 to calculate when the bed will become available. (Hint: it will be the date in cell B2 plus the number in cell B6. Use an absolute cell address.) Copy this formula to the other rows and columns.
4. Insert a COUNTIF function in cell I11 to count the number of instances a bed is free on the next day. (Hint: count the number of times that the date 2 Mar 2000 appears.)
5. Enhance the spreadsheet as you see fit. Print one copy of the completed spreadsheet.
6. Save the file as HOSP1.

Create the following letter, which will be sent to patients using the mailmerge facility:

> St John's Hospital
> Westpool
>
> Today's Date
>
> <NAME>
> <ADDRESS1>
> <ADDRESS2>
>
> Dear <NAME>,
>
> I note from our records that you are covered by medical insurance. I would be grateful if you could fill in the enclosed form and return it to your insurer.
>
> Dr <DOCTOR> will be in contact with you personally regarding professional fees.
>
> Sincerely,
>
> Your Name
> Hospital Administrator

1. Create the letter.
2. The mailmerge fields are shown. Link the mailmerge fields directly to the database.
3. Using the mailmerge facility, create letters for all patients who have medical insurance policies.
4. Print one of the letters.
5. Enhance the letter as you see fit.
6. Save the letter as HOSP.

'I think computer viruses should count as life. I think it says something about human nature that the only form of life we've created so far is purely destructive. We've created life in our own image.'
Stephen Hawking

Project 27

Most police forces around the world use IT in a variety of ways. Some of the more sophisticated uses include matching fingerprints or DNA samples using a database, using spreadsheets to help determine whether a fraud was committed etc. They use word processing to write reports.

Time   The estimated time for this project is two hours.

Rating   This project has a rating of five.

Skills   You need the following skills to successfully complete this project:

Software Package	Tasks to Complete	Explanations (see pages)
Spreadsheet	LOOKUP	145
Database	Index, copy	136
Word processing	Mailmerge with database	130

Project 27

DATABASE

The police use a database to track criminals. It includes information regarding their date of birth, address, type of crime etc. The database has the following structure:

FIELD NAME	WIDTH	DATATYPE	DESCRIPTION
NAME	12	Text	Prisoner's name
ADDRESS1	15	Text	First line of address
ADDRESS2	12	Text	Second line of address
DOA	8	Date	Date of arrest
PRISON	12	Text	Name of prison
TIME	2	Numeric	Length of sentence
CRIMES	25	Text	Crimes committed

Retrieve the file PRISON from the Web site. The database has the following structure:

NAME	ADDRESS1	ADDRESS2	DOA	PRISON	TIME	CRIMES
J Moon	1 Main St	Westpool	12/3/92	Mountjoy	10	Drugs, supply
L Star	2 East Pk	Jamestown	13/4/98	Wheatfield	6	Robbery
R Sunn	5 Long Tce	Eastpool	11/3/01	Mountjoy	4	Drugs, possession
P Lanet	23 West Pk	Eastpool	1/4/99	Wheatfield	7	Manslaughter
E Arth	5 West Rd	Jamestown	23/3/98	Mountjoy	6	Drugs, possession, robbery
S Oil	8 North Rd	Eastpool	15/4/00	Spike Is	2	Drunk driving
W East	4 East Pk	Westpool	7/3/01	Mountjoy	20	Murder
E West	12 Main St	Westpool	3/2/00	Wheatfield	12	Armed robbery
B Room	2 Left Lane	Jamestown	4/3/00	Spike Is	3	Breaking and entering
B Lanet	3 Park Ave	Jamestown	4/4/94	Mountjoy	9	Arson, robbery

1. Create an index using the DOA field as the primary key. Enhance the database as you see fit.
2. Insert this record using your own details:

Your name	Address	Address	4/4/98	Mountjoy	5	Robbery

3. Search for prisoners who have been jailed for crimes involving drugs.
4. Search for prisoners who were arrested between 1 January 1990 and 31 December 2000.
5. Sort the database using the PRISON field as the primary key and TIME as the secondary key. Print the results.
6. Copy all records of prisoners involved in robbery (armed or otherwise) to a new file and save it as ROBBERY.
7. Delete these records from the file PRISON.
8. Save the file as PRISON. Print only the NAME, PRISON, TIME and CRIMES fields.

Project 27

SPREADSHEET

This spreadsheet calculates police wages including overtime, taxes etc.

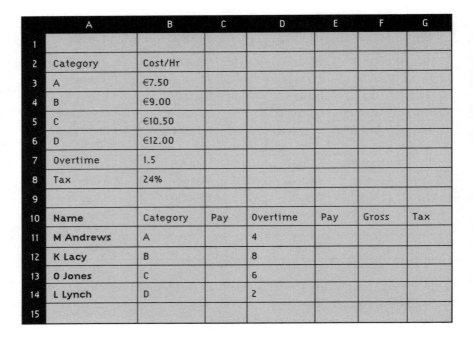

	A	B	C	D	E	F	G
1							
2	Category	Cost/Hr					
3	A	€7.50					
4	B	€9.00					
5	C	€10.50					
6	D	€12.00					
7	Overtime	1.5					
8	Tax	24%					
9							
10	Name	Category	Pay	Overtime	Pay	Gross	Tax
11	M Andrews	A		4			
12	K Lacy	B		8			
13	O Jones	C		6			
14	L Lynch	D		2			
15							

The categories refer to the length of service that a police officer has. The overtime rate is 1.5 (i.e. 1.5 multiplied by the number of hours of overtime multiplied by the hourly rate). The tax rate is assumed to be 24% for all officers.

1. Create the spreadsheet.
2. Using the LOOKUP function, determine the standard wage for all four employees in cells C11 to C14 (40 hours).
3. Using the LOOKUP function, determine the overtime for each employee. (Note: each employee is on a different pay rate.) Insert these values in cells E11 to E14.
4. Calculate the gross pay in cell F11. Copy the formula to the other cells in the column.
5. Determine the tax in cells G11 to G14.
6. In cell H10, insert the word *NET*. In cell H11, insert a formula to determine the net wage.
7. Save the file as PRISON, and print one copy.

Create the following letter, which will be sent to prisoners using the mailmerge facility:

Department of Justice
Westpool

Today's Date

<NAME>
<PRISON>

Dear <NAME>,

I note from the prison governor that your term in prison is two-thirds complete, and that your behaviour has been exemplary during that time.
I will therefore recommend to the parole board that you be released on licence at its next meeting.

Sincerely,

Your Name
Minister for Justice

'Old hackers never die. They just go to bitnet.'

Anon

1. Create the letter.
2. The mailmerge fields are shown. Link the mailmerge fields directly to the database.
3. Using the mailmerge facility, create letters for all prisoners who have completed two-thirds of their sentence.
4. Print one of the letters.
5. Enhance the letter as you see fit.
6. Save the letter as PRISON.

Project 28

IT plays an important part in school administration. Many schools keep records of student results on a database. They also use a database and word processor to send letters to the parents etc. Spreadsheets help the school administration to calculate salaries, expenses etc.

Time   The estimated time for this project is two hours.

Rating   This project has a rating of five.

Skills   You need the following skills to successfully complete this project:

Software Package	Tasks to Complete	Explanations (see pages)
Spreadsheet	LOOKUP	145
Database	Index	136
Word processing	Mailmerge with database	130

Project 28

DATABASE

The school uses a database to record student data. It includes information regarding their date of birth, address, telephone number etc. The database has the following structure:

FIELD NAME	WIDTH	DATATYPE	DESCRIPTION
SURNAME	10	Text	Student's surname
FIRST	10	Text	Student's first name
ADDRESS	15	Text	First line of address
TEL	7	Numeric	Telephone number
DOB	8	Date	Date of birth
CLASS	3	Text	Class name
DOCTOR	10	Text	Doctor's name

Retrieve the file SCHOOL. The database contains the following information. (Obviously, this is only a fraction of the size of an actual database.)

SURNAME	FIRST	ADDRESS	TEL	DOB	CLASS	DOCTOR
Lang	Brian	1 Main St	1132255	12/3/86	5A1	James
Long	James	23 Park St	1136653	2/5/89	2A2	Lovejoy
Lynch	Larry	31 Lark Tce	1135522	3/7/85	6A1	Spock
Lark	Mary	90 Kent St	1134421	6/2/86	5A2	Lovejoy
Lenny	Nuala	32 West St	1142535	12/6/87	3A1	James
Lyons	Claire	19 East Way	1146324	17/9/85	6A4	Lovejoy
Murphy	Mark	87 Brent Pk	1132778	19/4/86	5A2	Spock
Marks	Tara	54 College Pk	1138664	2/6/86	5A4	James
Martin	Joanne	32 Main St	1142683	12/4/85	6A6	Spock
Molloy	Beryl	12 Lark Tce	1147288	1/1/86	5A4	Lovejoy

1. Create an index using the SURNAME field as the primary key. Enhance it as you see fit.
2. Insert the following record using your own details:

Your Name		Your Address	1144421	Your DOB	5A2	Lovejoy

3. Search for students in year five. (Hint: their class name begins with 5.) Save this query as FIFTH.
4. B Molloy has left school. Remove this record from the database.
5. Search for students whose medical doctor is Lovejoy.
6. Insert a new field called DOC_TEL, which is the doctors' telephone number. The data is as follows:
   Lovejoy — 1134228, Spock — 1140933, James — 1130229
7. Insert another new field called PARENT/GUARDIAN and insert names for each parent or guardian.
8. Sort the database by SURNAME (primary key) and then by CLASS (secondary key).
9. Search for students born before 1988. Print only the NAME, DOB and CLASS fields for this query.
10. Print one copy of the complete database and save it as SCHOOL.

This spreadsheet calculates the receipts of a school musical using the LOOKUP function:

	A	B	C	D	E	F	G	H
1	School Musical							
2		Dress Rehearsal	Matinee	Evening				
3	Adult	€4.50	€5.00	€6.00				
4	Student	€2.00	€2.50	€3.00				
5	Child	€2.00	€2.00	€2.50				
6	OAP	€2.00	€2.50	€3.00				
7								
8	Attendance	Dress Rehearsal	Receipts	Monday Matinee	Receipts	Monday Evening	Receipts	Tuesday Evening
9	Adult	102		45		266		289
10	Student	245		150		255		279
11	Child	57		200		105		113
12	OAP	59		50		130		145
13								

1. Create the spreadsheet.
2. Enhance the column headings as you see fit.
3. Insert the word *Receipts* in cell I8.
4. Insert a formula in cell C9 using the LOOKUP function to calculate the total sales for adults at the dress rehearsal. Copy the formula to the cells in the other rows. Insert a similar formula for the receipts for the Monday matinee, Monday evening and Tuesday evening performances.
5. Format the receipts columns as currency values, which are accurate to two decimal places.
6. Insert the heading *Total* in cell J8. Insert a formula in J9 to add the receipts of all the performances. Copy this formula to the other rows.
7. Finally, create a chart showing the breakdown of the groups of people who attended each performance.
8. Save the file as SCHOOL and print one copy.

Create the following letter, which will be sent to the parents of fifth-year students reminding them of the no-smoking policy:

YOUR SCHOOL NAME
ADDRESS

<PARENT/GUARDIAN> <SURNAME>
<ADDRESS>
YOUR TOWN

Today's Date

Dear <PARENT/GUARDIAN> <SURNAME>,

I wish to remind you of the strict no-smoking policy in the school. It is illegal for children under sixteen years of age to smoke, and it is illegal for shops or others to sell them cigarettes. Apart from the legal implications there are the obvious health hazards associated with smoking. The medical evidence is overwhelming in this regard.

I would be failing in my duty as principal if I neglected this obvious area of concern. I hope that you will reinforce this message at home. The sanction for smoking in the school is two days' suspension.

Sincerely,

Your Name
Principal

1. Create the letter.
2. The mailmerge fields are shown. Link the mailmerge fields directly to the database.
3. Using the mailmerge facility, create letters for all fifth-year students.
4. Print one of the letters.
5. Enhance the letter as you see fit.
6. Print labels for the fifth-year students using the database as the data source. Use the FIRST, SURNAME and ADDRESS fields. Save the database as SCHOOL. Print one copy of the database.

Project 29

A recruitment company uses IT for all its business dealings:

- Databases to track employee and employer relationships
- Spreadsheets to calculate wages and commissions due to the company
- Word processing to send letters to its clients

Time   The estimated time for this project is two hours.

Rating   This project has a difficulty rating of five.

Skills   You need the following skills to successfully complete this project:

Software Package	Tasks to Complete	Explanations (see pages)
Spreadsheet	LOOKUP	145
Database	Labels	137
Word processing	Mailmerge with database	130

Project 29
DATABASE

The recruitment company uses many databases. This is an example of one of the databases, which it uses to target potential employees. It has the following structure:

FIELD NAME	WIDTH	DATATYPE	DESCRIPTION
NAME	12	Text	Name of employee
ADDRESS	12	Text	First line of address
TEL	7	Numeric	Telephone number
DOB	8	Date	Date of birth
FIELD	10	Text	Area of work
YRS	1	Numeric	No of years experience in this field
POSITION	15	Text	Present position

Retrieve the file RECRUIT. The database contains the following information. (This is only a small sample from an actual database.)

NAME	ADDRESS	TEL	DOB	FIELD	YRS	POS
M Molloy	12 Park St	2432255	12/3/76	Engineer	5	Snr Mechanical Engineer
J Coll	3 Main St	6653232	2/5/79	Computer	2	Network Administrator
P Burke	9 Wren Tce	4355228	3/7/75	Computer	3	Network Administrator
N Ferry	4 Clarke St	2434421	6/2/80	Engineer	3	Chemical Engineer
D O Loony	2 West St	2182535	12/6/77	Sales	5	Manager
S West	5 Park Way	2196324	17/9/81	Accountant	2	Certified Managerial
P Saunders	7 Brent Tce	2032778	19/4/82	Engineer	3	Process Engineer
O Quinn	5 College Pk	8438664	2/6/79	Sales	3	Manager
Y Reddy	2 Main St	9182683	12/4/75	Engineer	6	Senior Process Engineer
J Deer	81 Ridge St	7187288	1/1/80	Marketing	2	Manager

1. Sort the database on the FIELD (primary key) and YRS (secondary key) fields.
2. Insert the following record into the correct position in the database:

Your Name	1 Main St	8177288	1/1/80	Engineer	2	Process Engineer

3. Search for people with a background in engineering. Save this search as ENGINEER.
4. Using the previous query, search for people involved in process engineering only. Save this file as PROCESS.
5. Print labels for the process engineers listed in question four. The label must include the NAME and ADDRESS fields.
6. A company wants to recruit somebody for a managerial position. The company does not specify any particular discipline, but candidates must have at least four years' experience. Search for people who fulfil these criteria. Print only the NAME, YRS and POS fields. Save the file as RECRUIT and print one copy.

The recruitment company uses spreadsheets to calculate the commission due, based on each employee it recruits for each company. The fee is based on the equivalent of two weeks' salary for each employee, plus a fee based on the seniority of the position.

	A	B	C	D	E	F	G
1	A1 Recruitment						
2							
3	Position	Basic Fee					
4	Junior	€200					
5	Executive	€350					
6	Senior	€500					
7							
8	Company Name	Junior	Salary	Fee	Executive	Salary	Fee
9	Jacob Engineering	2	€18,900		3	€27,800	
10	LarkPharma	3	€17,600		1	€24,500	
11	Markson	1	€19,500		1	€26,900	
12	LogiCall	2	€18,900		2	€23,000	

1. Create the spreadsheet. Enhance it as you see fit.
2. Insert a formula using the LOOKUP function to calculate the fee for each company. The fee is calculated by adding two weeks' salary to the basic fee.
3. Insert the following data into the spreadsheet:

Name	Senior	Salary	Fee
Jacob Engineering	2	€38,700	
LarkPharma	3	€37,200	
Markson	1	€39,800	
LogiCall	2	€41,500	

4. Insert the relevant formula to calculate the fee using the LOOKUP function.
5. Insert a TOTAL column and calculate the total fee for each company. Save the file as RECRUIT and print one copy.

The following letter will be sent to the process engineers who fulfilled the criteria in the database:

A1 Recruitment Ltd
Embassy House

<NAME>
<ADDRESS>

Today's Date

Dear <NAME>,

I am delighted to inform you that you have been selected for interview for the post of Assistant Senior Engineer in a large pharmaceutical company.

I have forwarded your CV to the Head of Human Resources who will be conducting the interview herself.

I would request that you attend for interview on Monday 12th. Please telephone or e-mail me to arrange a specific time. If this date is unsuitable, please let me know as soon as possible and I will try to reschedule your interview.

Sincerely,

J Tenterdon
Human Resources

1. Create the letter.
2. The mailmerge fields are shown. Link the mailmerge fields directly to the database.
3. Using the mailmerge facility, create letters for all process engineers.
4. Print one of these letters.
5. Enhance the letter as you see fit.
6. Save the letter as RECRUIT.

Project 30

A veterinary practice uses IT in the following ways:

- It uses a database to track farmers, livestock, etc.
- It uses spreadsheets to create accounts for each farmer.
- It uses word processing to send letters to the farmers.

Time   The estimated time for this project is two hours.

Rating   This project has a rating of five.

Skills   You need the following skills to successfully complete this project:

Software Package	Tasks to Complete	Explanations (see pages)
Spreadsheet	LOOKUP	145
Database	Index	136
Word processing	Mailmerge with database	130

Project 30
DATABASE

The veterinary practice uses a database to help track livestock testing in their area. The database includes the farmer's name and address, the number of livestock etc. The structure of the database is as follows:

FIELD NAME	WIDTH	DATATYPE	DESCRIPTION
ACCOUNT	6	Alphanumeric	Account number
NAME	12	Text	Name of employee
ADDRESS	12	Text	First line of address
TEL	6	Numeric	Telephone number
LAST	8	Date	Date of last test
TYPE	10	Text	Type of test
BREED	10	Text	Type of animal

Retrieve the file VET. The database contains the following information:

ACCOUNT	NAME	ADDRESS	TEL	LAST	TYPE	BREED
A11224	J Smith	Maherroe	224566	12/3/00	TB	Mixed
A11225	W Alcorn	Cranfield	225446	3/4/00	TB	Limousin
B11545	L Henry	Maherroe	224573	5/2/00	Lambing	Suffolk
B11558	P Joyce	Cranfield	225876	30/5/00	TB	Mixed
A11226	M Locke	Woodquarter	226778	19/3/00	Calving	Charolais
C11655	R Roberts	Woodquarter	226548	12/4/00	TB	Charolais
D11557	P Mulcahy	Maherroe	224865	15/3/00	Lambing	Suffolk
C11656	M Martin	Cranfield	225877	10/2/00	TB	Mixed
B11546	O Clancy	Cranfield	225687	4/3/00	Lambing	Charolais
C11657	D Daniels	Woodquarter	226891	12/3/00	Lambing	Suffolk

1. Create an index using the ACCOUNT field as the primary key.
2. Insert the following record into the correct position in the database:

A11300	Your name	Woodquarter	226895	19/3/00	Lambing	Suffolk

3. Search for all farmers who had TB testing carried out during the year.
4. M Locke has sold her farm to O Kelly, Maherroe. Make the necessary changes.
5. Search for TB testing that did not involve a mixed herd.
6. Search for all veterinary activities in March 2000. Print the results of this search using your name as a header.
7. Add a new field called PAID, which is a Yes/No type field. Insert the following data: Y, Y, Y, N, N, Y, N, Y, N, N, N.
8. Search for farmers who have not settled their accounts yet.
9. Print the entire database and save it as VET.

The veterinary practice uses a spreadsheet to calculate the fees owed by each farmer. The spreadsheet uses the LOOKUP function to calculate the fee to charge, which depends on the type of work carried out. (Work carried out in the surgery is not included in this spreadsheet.)

	A	B	C	D	E	F
1						
2	Work	Fee				
3	TB test	€1.20				
4	Lamb scan	€0.60				
5	Calf scan	€5.80				
6	Standard callout	€16.00				
7						
8	Name	Work	No	Fee	Vat @ 21%	Total
9	P Joyce	TB	50			
10	W Alcorn	Lamb Scan	49			
11	L Henry	Calf Scan	12			
12	D Daniels	TB	35			
13	M Martin	Calf Scan	45			

1. Create the spreadsheet as shown above. Enhance it as you see fit.
2. Insert a formula using the LOOKUP function to calculate the fee for each farmer. (Note: include the standard callout fee of €16.00.)
3. Insert a formula to add VAT at 21% to the fee.
4. Insert a formula to calculate the total fee for each farmer i.e. the fee plus VAT.
5. Save the file as VET and print one copy.

'The most likely way for the world to be destroyed, most experts agree, is by accident. That's where we come in; we're computer professionals. We cause accidents.'

Nathaniel Borenstein

The following letter will be sent to the farmers who have not paid their bills yet:

Johnson and Williams Veterinary Practice
Milltown Road
Westpool

<NAME>
<ADDRESS>

Monday 7 July

Dear <NAME>,

I refer to our recent services on your farm for which we have not yet been paid.

I enclose an invoice, which I would appreciate if you could pay in full by Friday 12 July.

Late payment causes difficulties for all of us. I would appreciate your urgent attention to this matter.

Sincerely,

M Johnson

1. Create the letter.
2. The mailmerge fields are shown. Link the mailmerge fields directly to the database.
3. Using the mailmerge facility, create letters for all farmers who have not paid their bills yet.
4. Insert a copy of the spreadsheet invoice that was created previously. (Note: include the details only of the farmer you are writing to.)
5. Print one of the letters.
6. Create labels for the letters using the NAME and ADDRESS fields. Save the file as VET and print one copy of the labels.

Part 2 Concepts

You are probably already familiar with the following terms in word processing:

Cut, Copy, PASTE

- CUT — Means to select a block of text and remove it from its current position. A copy is kept in the computer's memory.
- COPY — Means to select a block of text and copy it to another position. So, there are two copies of the selected text.
- PASTE — Means to take the copied text and put it into its new position.

These terms come from old printing terms when the text was *cut*, using scissors, and *pasted* to its new position, using gum.

Using LINKS

Another feature that you can use when pasting text is to link it with the original copied text. Any changes that are made to the source (original) copy are automatically made in the new copy. As you can imagine, this is especially useful when updating a report or a document, because it means that you have to update only the source text. Any changes will be reflected in the copied text. These links can occur in the same or in different documents.

Find out how to paste a link in the word processing package you are using. Then try the following exercise:

> In a new report issued today, the government said that there will be 200 extra vacancies in the Civil Service. This is more than twice the original estimate.
> 1. Type the previous paragraph and copy it.
> 2. Paste the paragraph using a link. Change 200 to 400 in the source paragraph.

A font is the typeface displayed on the screen when you type. There are many different kinds of fonts, for example:

- This is TIMES NEW ROMAN.
- This is COURIER.
- This is ARIAL.
- This is COMIC SANS MS.

You can select the text, and then easily change the size of the font. The new font is then displayed on the screen or on the printout.

Fonts are described as being either proportional or non-proportional. In other words, the letters and characters that make up the font are either in proportion to each other or not. If you look at the characters in this sentence, you see that some letters take up more space than others. For example, the character *W* takes up more space than the character *I*, this is because the font is a proportional one. In a non-proportional font, the characters take up the same amount of space regardless of width. Therefore, the character *W* takes up the same amount of space as the character *I*. An easy way of checking whether a font is proportional or not is to type five Ws on one line and five Is on the line below. If they are equal in size, then the font is non-proportional:

What Are

Proportional and

Non-Proportional

Fonts?

WWWWW
IIIII
This is a proportional font —
Times New Roman.

WWWWW
IIIII
This is a non-proportional font —
Courier.

What Are Serif and Sanserif Fonts?

Fonts can also be described as being either serif or sanserif. Look at the following two letters:

The letter on the left is a serif font. The serifs are the 'drops' at each end of the cross bar, and at the bottom of the T. Serifs are designed to make reading text easier.

The *T* on the right-hand side is sanserif (*sans* means *without*). As you can see, it is plain type, simply two bars without any embellishments.

Try the following questions:

1. Which of the following is a non-proportional, serif font?

   a) **embellishment**
   b) **embellishment**
   c) embellishment
   d) embellishment

2. Which of the following is a proportional, sanserif font?

   a) embellishment
   b) embellishment
   c) embellishment
   d) embellishment

3. Which of the following is a proportional, serif font?

   a) **embellishment**
   b)**embellishment**
   c) embellishment
   d) embellishment

Formatting a page refers to the way you can change the layout of the page. You can do this in a number of different ways.

What Is
FORMATTING?

The orientation of a page refers to the way the page is facing when it is printed. This page is orientated in a *portrait* direction. If you turn the book on its side, it is orientated in a *landscape* direction. Portrait is used more commonly than landscape. Landscape is useful when you want to print a lot of text on one page, or for printing spreadsheets when you can print many columns of data on one page.

What Is
ORIENTATION?

The page margins refer to the space between the edge of the paper and the beginning of the text. There are four margins called: top, bottom, left and right. The spacing is usually measured in either inches or centimetres. By changing the margins, you can change the layout of the page.

What Are
MARGINS?

Portrait   Landscape

A header is graphics or text that appears in the top margin of every page e.g. the chapter number.

What Is a Header?

A footer is graphics or text that appears in the bottom margin of each page e.g. the page number.

What Is a Footer?

One of the easiest ways to format text is to use **bold**, *italic* or <u>underline</u>. Be careful not to overdo it. Use these features only to enhance your work.

What Is TABULATION?

Tabulation refers to the way you can make text 'jump' across the screen without using the spacebar. The tab key is located above the Caps Lock key, and has two arrows pointing in opposite directions. Tabs are useful when you want to line objects up on screen e.g. columns of figures. You can determine how far the text moves by setting the tabs at different distances. Tabs are normally pre-set at 0.5 of an inch. Never use the spacebar to align text, it wastes time and rarely works. The text may appear straight on screen, but invariably the text on the printout will not be aligned correctly. Look at the following examples:

Example A

A	B
1,000	1,200
1,200	1,300
1,300	1,400

Example B

A	B
1,000	1,200
1,200	1,300
1,300	1,400

Example A uses tabs to align the text. The result is that both columns are straight. Example B uses the spacebar to align the text. The result is that column B is crooked.

What Is INDENTATION?

Indented text is offset against the left or right margin by a certain distance. Indents can be left, right or hanging. This paragraph uses a left indent.

A hanging indent is where the first line of each paragraph starts further to the right than the rest of the paragraph. The first line in this paragraph uses a hanging indent.

A superscript is text that is raised slightly above the normal line of text e.g. r^2. The 2 is a superscript. A subscript is text that is placed below the normal line of text e.g. H_2O. The 2 in this instance is a subscript.

Line spacing refers to the distance between the lines of text. Most text is spaced automatically at single-line spacing such as this text. However, some reports, especially scientific reports, always use double line spacing.

Many authors submit their work in double-line spacing, because it makes it

easier for the editor to mark changes in the text. This paragraph is set in

double-line spacing.

You can specify the space between lines (single or double) in values between 1.5, 1.25, 1.75 etc. When changing the line spacing, it is easier to type the text normally, select the text you want to change, and then change the line spacing. Do not put in blank lines manually, the computer will do this automatically.

Find out how to change the line spacing on the word processing package that you use.

What Is a PROTECTED SPACE?

Far from being controlled by the Star-Ship Federation, protected spaces are useful to prevent word wrap in the middle of dates or words that you do not want to be separated at the end of a sentence. For example, 12 September 2000 will be broken into the separate components, 12 September 2000 like this by word wrap. You may want to display the entire date on one line. To do this, you must use protected spaces between *12* and *September*, and between *September* and *2000*. In this way, the date behaves as one long word and is displayed on one line only.

Bullets and NUMBERING

When creating a list of items with your word processor, you can get the computer to automatically create a numbered list 1, 2, 3 etc., or a, b, c etc., or a bulleted list. Bullets are small dots before each item in a list. For example:

- Item 1
- Item 2
- Item 3
- Item 4

1 Item 1
2 Item 2
3 Item 3
4 Item 4

Using COLUMNS

You can use columns of text in newsletters or flyers. Columns are useful because many readers are already familiar with the typical newspaper layout of a page. They can also easily lead the eye using headings in bold to points of interest.

Placing clip art or a graphic within the columns is easy and attracts the eye. Sometimes a caption is displayed under the graphic describing it. It is easy to format the graphic to appear within a defined box, or you can make the text wrap around it.

The number of columns can vary depending on the paper size and column width. Too many columns can lead to a narrow column width, which can make the text difficult to read.

Most word processing packages have a facility called Find/Replace. This allows the user to search for a word or a date and replace it with a different word or date. It can also replace numbers. It saves time when editing, because the computer automatically changes the words. You can also use Find/Replace in databases and spreadsheets.

Form fields are used in word processing to create a point in a document where the user can insert data. The user cannot insert data in any other part of the document, only in the form field. Form fields are used in documents that require little change. Many solicitors use standard letters containing form fields. An advantage of using form fields is that the main document is protected from change, while users can still enter data. This is especially important in legal or medical letters. In the following example, the DATE and NAME fields are the only parts of the document where you can enter data. This minimises the risk of error. It is also more efficient, because you do not have to retype the letter.

Using the FIND/REPLACE FACILITY

What Are FORM FIELDS?

LegalEagles Ltd
LegalEagle House

<DATE>

Dear <NAME>,

Thank you for your letter of <DATE> inst. Further to our client's instructions we require a full medical report on our client's injuries.

We remain

W Johnson

Solicitor

MAILMERGE?

This is one of the most powerful features of a word processor. It allows you to create a standard document, for example, a letter, with another document containing variables. The variables replace the data in the standard document. The following are examples of the types of variables:

VARIABLE	DESCRIPTION	EXAMPLE
FNAME	The first name of the person you are sending the document to	John
SNAME	The surname	Molloy
LINE1	First address line	12 High Street
LINE2	Second address line	Morecambe

Two files are created: the data file, which contains all the data that replaces the variables, and the main document.

Data File

The following is an example of a data file:

FNAME	SNAME	LINE1	LINE2
Martin	Clarke	12 Main St	Westpool
Susan	Finch	23 Park Tce	Jamestown
Grace	Reddy	2 Cottage Rd	Carrokeel

Main Document

This is an example of a main document:

```
<FNAME> <SNAME>
<LINE1>
<LINE2>
Dear <FNAME>,
Text
```

When you merge these two documents, the data in the data file replaces the variables in the main document. This allows a standard letter to appear as if it were typed specially for the recipient. Mailmerge is used extensively to produce documents that appear as if they were created specifically for each individual.

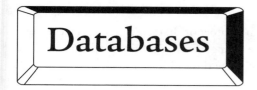

Databases

Databases are collections of organised data from which you can easily retrieve information. Simple examples of databases include a telephone directory or a library. A telephone directory is organised by code (e.g. the 01 directory) and then by surname. Looking up a telephone number is a simple task when you know the surname and address. Try to imagine the reverse scenario i.e. trying to find a person's name when you know the phone number! A library is a more advanced database; books are organised by topic, and then by author.

The information in a database is divided into two main areas: fields and records. A field contains the same type of information e.g. age, first name etc. A record contains all the data relating to an item e.g. first name, surname, age, date of birth etc.

SURNAME	FIRST	ADDRESS	TEL	DOB
Lang	Brian	1 Main St	1132255	12/3/86
Long	James	23 Park St	1136653	2/5/89
Lynch	Larry	31 Lark Tce	1135522	3/7/85

This database consists of five fields: SURNAME, FIRST, ADDRESS, TEL and DOB. It has three records: one for Brian Lang, another for James Long and one for Larry Lynch. Columns can be thought of as fields, while rows can be thought of as records.

Fields can be of different types e.g. a field containing dates of births is called a date field.

DATATYPE	DESCRIPTION	EXAMPLE
TEXT	Contains text only	John
NUMERIC	Contains numbers only	01 11234
ALPHANUMERIC	Contains a mixture of text and numbers	A11222
DATE	Contains dates	27/03/66
CURRENCY	Contains money/currency values	$12.34

Field Width   The width of a field is the maximum number of characters that it can contain. A field width of five contains the name Barry (5), but it cannot contain Martin (6). Luckily, you can easily change the width of a field.

What Is a DATA ENTRY FORM?

When looking at or entering data in a database, it is sometimes easier to enter data using a data entry form. A data entry form shows all the information for one record at a time. On the other hand, you can view the data as a list where all the records are displayed. Data entry forms make it easier to enter data:

```
┌─────────────────────────────────────────────────────┐
│          Markham Library Database                   │
│                                                      │
│   Author:    _____      Title:      _____    │
│   Copies:    _____      Date Out:   _____    │
│   Returned:  _____      Borrower:   _____    │
│                                                      │
│   Record 1 of 500                                    │
└─────────────────────────────────────────────────────┘
```

Adding/Deleting FIELDS OR RECORDS

Sometimes you may want to add or delete a field. When adding a field, pay close attention to the datatype and width. If you delete a field, all the information in that field will be deleted, so be careful!

It is more usual to add or delete a record and make changes to a record's information. Adding a record is simple. You just fill in a data entry form with the relevant information. When removing a record you remove all the information within that record.

Sorting a DATABASE

A database can be sorted in a number of ways, for example, alphabetically, numerically etc. Sorts are described as being either ascending or descending. If you sort the letters A – Z in ascending order, they are arranged as A, B, C, D, E etc. If you sort them in descending order, they are arranged as Z, Y, X, W, V etc.

Key Field   The field on which a database is sorted is called the key field.

A database can be sorted on more than one field. This is called multilevel sorting. Instead of having just one key field, two are used.

Doing

Multilevel Sorts

The first field to be sorted is called the primary key field. The second field to be sorted is called the secondary key field.

Primary Key Field

Example

NAME	AGE	GENDER
JOHN	15	M
MARY	16	F
SHANE	17	M
GRACE	17	F
IVOR	18	M

If this database is sorted using the GENDER field as the primary key and the AGE field as the secondary key, the database will be sorted firstly on GENDER and then on AGE. The sorted database is as follows:

NAME	AGE	GENDER
MARY	16	F
GRACE	17	F
JOHN	15	M
SHANE	17	M
IVOR	18	M

As you can see, the database is sorted using the GENDER field first; all the females are together and all the males are together. Then the database is sorted by AGE e.g. the record for JOHN comes before SHANE or IVOR, because he is the youngest.

Searching a database for information is the main purpose for creating and using a database. For example, you need to know the following:

• What information you seek
• What field the information is in

Look at the following example of a database of candles produced in a candle factory:

Example

NAME	DATE	DESCRIPTION	QUANTITY	PRICE
FLOOD	12/7	White, scented	5	€14.50
JOHNSON	13/7	White, scented	4	€14.50
O' HARA	14/7	Beeswax, unscented	4	€20.00
MCELWEE	19/6	Beeswax, scented	3	€18.00
MCCALLUM	12/6	Blue, unscented	3	€14.50
SWEENEY	18/7	Marbled, unscented	5	€14.50
GRIER	13/6	Blue, scented	3	€15.50
KERR	23/7	Marbled, scented	4	€16.00
MARTIN	21/6	White, scented	6	€14.50
FIRTH	22/7	White, scented	4	€14.50

Suppose you want a list of candles costing €14.50. This information is in the PRICE field. You write the query as PRICE=14.50. Only records matching this criterion will be listed.

Suppose you want to list unscented candles. This information is in the DESCRIPTION field. The query reads: DESCRIPTION contains UNSCENTED.

Using the AND

Query

Sometimes you might like to ask a multipart question e.g. list those candles at €14.50 that are also unscented. In this case, there are two criteria to fulfil: the candle must cost €14.50 and it must be unscented. Therefore, the query reads: PRICE=14.50 *and* DESCRIPTION contains UNSCENTED. Only those records that fulfil both these criteria are listed.

What if you want to create the following query: list all candles that are greater than €14.00 or scented. Again, there are two parts to this question. In this case, however, if a record fulfils either one of the parts it is listed. If it is greater than €14.00, or if it is scented. Therefore this query reads as follows: PRICE>14.00 *or* DESCRIPTION contains SCENTED.

If you want the database to list all candles that do not cost €14.50, then you use the operator NOT. This query reads as follows: PRICE NOT 14.50.

Using OR and NOT

Many common mathematical functions can be easily used on fields e.g. fields can be added together, multiplied, divided or subtracted from each other. Obviously the field cannot contain text and must be either a numerical or currency field. Most database packages will carry out common statistical functions such as average, mean, total etc. on fields. Look at the following example:

Using

**MATHS ON
FIELDS**

PRODUCT	NET	VAT	RETAIL
BREAD	0.70		
SUGAR (1 kg)	0.90		
TEA (180 bags)	2.80		
JAM	0.95		
MILK (2 L)	1.80		

You can insert a formula in the VAT field to calculate the VAT on the price of the product. This formula reads: =NET*21%. This means multiply the price in the NET field by 21%. You can enter another formula in the RETAIL field to add the VAT to the NET price. This formula then reads: =NET+VAT. This formula adds the price in the NET field to the calculated VAT.

Using an
INDEX

Another method of sorting a database is to create an index. A database index is similar to an index in a book showing where each topic (record) is located. The following example shows a database where the records are indexed in ascending order using the NAME field:

No	NAME
1	Beryl
2	Mary
3	Eithne
4	Anne
5	Caroline

Database

No
4
1
5
3
2

Index

No	NAME
4	Anne
1	Beryl
5	Caroline
3	Eithne
2	Mary

Output

As you can see, the index file consists only of the record numbers and not the actual records. This means that an index file is usually small and therefore easily updated. The output shows the records as they appear in the database.

When a new record is added to the database the index is automatically updated, and the record is inserted in the correct position. This illustrates an important difference between indexing a database and sorting a database. If the database was sorted in the normal way, the new record would be added at the end of the database, and the database would no longer be sorted.

Using the
FIND/REPLACE
FACILITY

The Find/Replace facility in a database is the same as the Find/Replace facility in word processing. You can choose to replace text or numbers in a field or in the complete database. This makes it useful for replacing data quickly and efficiently in the entire database.

When a database contains the names and addresses of individuals, you can use this data to create labels for mailing purposes. You can arrange the labels in a variety of ways on a page, depending on the label size.

Example

NAME	ADDRESS1	ADDRESS2
J Smith	1 Main St	Westpool
I Williams	2 Market Sq	Milford
K Lucy	15 Woodstown Dale	Knocklyon
P Burke	44 Canny Pk	Sligo
J Martin	23 Abbey St	Jamestown
A Grier	178 James Tce	Williamstown
A Sweeney	43 Westpark Way	Milford
S Kerr	18 New Park	Jamestown

You can create labels using the previous information and arrange them two-across the page as follows:

J Smith
1 Main St
Westpool

I Williams
2 Market Sq
Milford

K Lucy
15 Woodstown Dale
Knocklyon

P Burke
44 Canny Pk
Sligo

Most database applications have built-in wizards or label generators to help simplify the task of creating labels. You can choose to insert or remove fields according to the type of information you want to appear on the label.

Generating REPORTS

Many databases have a facility to allow the user to create a report on the information in the database. This allows you to design the page e.g. insert a header or footer, and to show which fields you want to insert in the report. Most report generators allow the user to add the contents of a field.

Example

Report on Sales for First Quarter

By John Kennedy

Name	Region	Sales	Price
K Nugent	A	1,200	€10,090
L Harvey	B	1,344	€12,288
B Ryan	A	1,233	€15,449
I Lynch	C	1,566	€18,990
P Peters	A	1,099	€12,779
S Waters	B	1,227	€13,356
Total		7,669	€82,952

Linking DATABASES

Another powerful feature of databases is their ability to be linked to each other. You can do this by specifying a particular field in which to establish the link between the databases. This field is normally the primary key field e.g. the record number.

Example

NO	FIRST_NAME
1	John
2	Mary
3	Claire

NO	SURNAME
1	Kelly
2	Martin
3	Rogers

This simple example shows only the record number and one field from each database. However, it does show how they are linked using the record number field.

Spreadsheets

A spreadsheet is divided into cells into which you can insert information. The information may be text, numbers or formulas. Each cell has a unique address, which is determined by the column letter and row number that the cell is in.

The following spreadsheet includes examples of cells containing text, numbers and formulas. The cell B1 contains 'Week1', C3 contains 1,300 and D2 contains the formula to add the contents of cells B2 and C2. Normally, only the results of a formula are shown and not the formula itself.

	A	B	C	D
1	Sales	Week1	Week2	Total
2	Peters	1,200	1,100	=B2+C2
3	Lee	1,250	1,300	=B3+C3
4	Total	=B2+B3	=C2+C3	

You can also see that row 1 is in bold font. It is easy to enhance the appearance of a spreadsheet, using different fonts, sizes or colours. You can also insert or delete rows or columns to create a better visual impact. The previous example has been modified with blank rows and columns as follows:

	A	B	C	D	E
1	Sales	Week1	Week2		Total
2					
3	Peters	1,200	1,100		=B3+C3
4	Lee	1,250	1,300		=B4+C4
5					
6	Total	=B3+B4	=C3+C4		

This spreadsheet is easier to look at, and the results are easier to see at a glance. Notice also that the formulas automatically change when rows or columns are inserted or deleted.

Formatting
CELLS

You can format cells to show data in a variety of ways e.g. currency, percentage, date, time etc. This allows the data to be interpreted easily. You can also format rows or columns of cells as follows:

	A	B	C	D
1	Region	Sales	Amount	Date
2	A	1,200	$12,340.10	12/3/00
3	B	1,250	$12,609.89	13/4/00
4	C	1,100	$11,490.34	15/4/00

The figures in column B are formatted to number values, which are accurate to zero decimal places. Column C has been formatted to currency values, which are accurate to two decimal places, whereas column D has been formatted to date.

Changes in Column Width

You can easily change the column width in a spreadsheet. You can change the width of a column globally i.e. throughout the spreadsheet, or locally i.e. within the selected column. If a column isn't wide enough to show all the data, an error message is displayed.

Inserting
ROWS OR COLUMNS

By inserting blank rows or columns, you can visually enhance a spreadsheet as in the following example:

	A	B	C	D	E
1	Sales	Week1	Week2		Total
2					
3	Peters	1,200	1,100		=B3+C3
4	Lee	1,250	1,300		=B4+C4
5					
6	Total	=B3+B4	=C3+C4		

Notice that the formulas automatically change when rows or columns are inserted or deleted.

When you enter a formula in a cell, you can copy it to another column or row. The computer automatically changes the formula to take account of the new cells. Take the following example:

	A	B	C	D
1		Number	Price	Total
2	Week2	50	€1.45	=B2*C2
3	Week3	45	€1.56	=B3*C3
4	Week4	54	€1.45	=B4*C4

In cell D2, there is a formula to multiply the contents of B2 by the value in C2. Now look at the formulas in D3 and D4. The only difference between each formula is the row number. Therefore, if you enter only the formula in D2, you can copy this formula to cells D3 and D4 and the computer makes the necessary changes for you. This is called relative copying.

You have seen how the computer changes a formula automatically when it is copied from one column or row to another. Sometimes you may not want a formula to change; you may want it to remain the same. This is called an absolute address. Look at the following example:

	A	B	C	D
1	VAT	21%		
2				
3	Camera	Cost	Vat	Total
4	Pentax	€250	=B4*$B$1	=B4+C4
5	Olympus	€90	=B5*$B$1	=B5+C5
6	Canon	€150	=B6*$B$1	=B6+C6

Look at the formula in C4. The dollar sign ($) denotes an absolute cell address. This means that you can copy this formula, but only the first part of the formula (the B4 part) changes. However, the second part of the formula ($B$1) does not change. This is because the second part is an absolute cell address.

In this example, a company wants to pay their employees a bonus, but only if they sell a certain quantity of items during a four-week period. The company wants a spreadsheet to calculate whether a bonus is paid.

	A	B	C	D	E	F	G
1	ACME Sales						
2		Week1	Week2	Week3	Week4	Total	Bonus
3	Jones	12	11	13	14		
4	Smith	11	9	8	8		
5	Roberts	13	8	9	10		
6	Young	12	11	11	14		
7	Green	13	12	14	13		
8							

A bonus is paid only if the employee sells more than forty items during a four-week period. If employees sell more than forty items, they receive a bonus of €100; otherwise, they do not receive any bonus. In cell F3, you insert a formula to calculate the total sold during the four-week period. You then copy the formula to the other rows. In cell G3, you must insert a formula to determine whether a bonus is due, and if so, what that bonus will be. You use the IF function as follows:

=IF(F3>40, 100, 0)

This reads as follows: if F3 is greater than 40, then insert the value 100, otherwise insert 0 (zero). The IF function is generally written as follows:

=IF(CONDITION, TRUE, FALSE)

The condition can use the following symbols:

- > (greater than)
- < (less than)
- >=(greater than or equal to)
- <= (less than or equal to)
-   = (equal to)
- <> (not equal to)

The IF function has variations, one of these is using AND with IF. This is similar to using AND in a database — two conditions must be satisfied. The general format for using IF with AND is as follows:

=IF(AND(CONDITION1, CONDITION2), TRUE, FALSE)

This reads as follows: if condition one is true and condition two is true, then apply TRUE, otherwise apply FALSE.

Using OR with IF is similar in structure, instead of AND, use OR. This is written as follows:

=IF(OR(CONDITION1, CONDITION2), TRUE, FALSE)

This reads as follows: if condition one is true or condition two is true, then apply TRUE, otherwise apply FALSE.

Look at the following example:

	A	B	C	D
1	ACME Sales			
2				
3	Name	Service	Sales	Bonus
4	M Burns	22	240	
5	W Smithers	35	245	
6	N Flanders	40	287	
7	R Lovejoy	21	254	
8	C Wiggam	30	247	

The company wants to create a loyalty and incentive scheme for its employees. Employees get a bonus of €100 if they have twenty-five or more months' service *and* sales of 250 or more. Otherwise, they get nothing. The formula is as follows:

=IF(AND(B4>=25, C4>=250),100,0)

The company wants more employees to get the bonus to boost morale. So, now employees get a bonus if they have twenty-five or more months' service *or* sales of 250 or more. The formula is as follows:

=IF(OR(B4>=25, C4>=250),100,0)

The COUNT function counts how many numbers are in a range. It ignores cells that contain text. Take the following example:

	A	B	C	D
1	ACME PRINT			
2		Sales	Profit	
3	Monday	122	€2,334	
4	Tuesday	134	€2,431	
5	Wednesday	n/a	n/a	
6	Thursday	233	€4,225	
7	Friday	188	€3,775	
8				

If you insert a formula in B8 to count the number values in the range B2 to B7, it looks like the following:

=COUNT(B2:B7)

It returns the value 4, because it ignores *sales* and *n/a*.

If you want to include text, you use the COUNTA function. It includes everything except blank cells. You write the function as follows:

=COUNTA(B2:B7)

It returns a value of 6, because it includes *sales* and *n/a*.

Perhaps the most impressive of the COUNT functions is COUNTIF. This function counts the number of times a number or text appears in a range. For example:

=COUNTIF(B2:C7, "n/a")

This function returns the value 2, because there are two instances where n/a occurs in the range B2 to C7.

The LOOKUP function is a useful tool in spreadsheets. It allows the spreadsheet to lookup a code or value and insert the relevant value associated with the code. Take the following example:

	A	B	C	D
1	ACME Design			
2				
3	Code	Price		
4	A112	€1.23		
5	B334	€2.56		
6	C445	€1.67		
7				
8				
9	Name	Code	Quantity	Total
10	S Kerr	A112	24	
11	M McHugh	A112	12	
12	K Johnson	C445	14	

The range A3 to B6 is called the lookup table, where the program looks for information. You can insert a formula in cell D10 to calculate how much S Kerr has to pay by using a lookup function. The formula is as follows:

=LOOKUP(B10,$A$3:$B$6)*C10

This reads as follows: lookup the data in cell B10 (A112) in the range A3 to B6, and insert the data associated with it (1.23), then multiply this value by C10.

Note that the lookup range is referred to using absolute cell addresses, which means it can be copied.

The Internet

History of
THE INTERNET

The Internet has existed since the 1960s when the RAND Corporation developed it in the USA. The RAND Corporation was a military 'think-tank'. The problem they faced was how to create a military communications network that would survive a direct attack, for example, in a nuclear war? A nuclear strike would decimate any computer network. The command and control centre of the network would be a primary target for a nuclear strike. If the control centre were hit, the whole network would collapse.

They eventually arrived at a possible solution. The network would not have a central authority; it would be designed to operate while in tatters. Information would be divided into packets that would be sent individually from one part of the network to another, not necessarily using the same route. If part of the network were down, then the packets would be switched to another route. So many routes would be available that it would be highly unlikely that a message could not be delivered. The order in which the packets were sent or received did not matter, because they could be put together in the correct sequence at the destination.

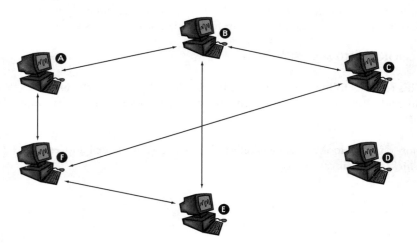

In the previous figure, computer A wants to send a message to computer E. Part of the message may travel along A – B – E, another part might travel A – B – C – F – E. You can see that although computer D is disconnected, this does not disrupt the message. Remove computer F and see how many ways the message can travel.

Each computer on the network was called a node. In 1969 there were only four nodes on the network. The network was called ARPANET (Advanced Research Projects Agency). By 1972 there were thirty-seven nodes on the network. Most of the traffic was from researchers exchanging messages on projects and sending personal messages. Little high-level computing was done!

By 1977, ARPANET was using TCP/IP as its primary network protocol. TCP stands for *Transmission Control Protocol*, which breaks up information into packets, and then reassembles them at their destination. IP stands for *Internet Protocol*, which handles how the packets are addressed and sent along the nodes. TCP/IP is the standard protocol used today with the Internet.

What Is TCP/IP?

ARPANET steadily increased in size with more and more networks joining. By 1983 the military section broke away from ARPANET to become MILNET. ARPANET was now only a small subsection of what became known as the Internet.

'The Internet is like a giant jellyfish. You can't step on it. You can't go around it. You've got to get through it.'
John Evans

Each node had its own abbreviation depending on its function. For example, this is a list of abbreviations:
• Military nodes used *.mil*
• Government departments used *.gov*
• Educational establishments used *.edu*
• Commercial enterprises used *.com*
• Non-profit organisations used *.org*
• Networks used *.net*

From its early beginnings as a military communications tool, the Internet developed rapidly to become a gigantic library of information unparalleled in the history of mankind. Most of this information is free! Today millions of people worldwide use the Internet. Now let's look at what you need before you start.

To connect to the Internet you need to have access to the following:
• Computer
• Modem
• Telephone line
• ISP

The computer can communicate only via a modem (which is short for *modulator demodulator*). The modem converts the computer signals into signals that can be carried over a telephone line and vice versa. Internet charges vary, but usually you only pay a local-call rate.

What Is AN ISP?

You will also need to sign up with an ISP (Internet Service Provider). Basically the ISP provides the user with the software and an account to enable the user to connect to the Internet. The account consists of a login name and a password. Normally the ISP provides a certain amount of Web space for hosting your own homepages and a few free e-mail addresses. Now you're ready to surf!

Apart from the Web, the Internet also consists of electronic mail (e-mail), USENET, file transfer and on-line chat. Let's look at e-mail first.

Electronic MAIL

Electronic mail or e-mail is one of the most common features of the Internet. You can send text messages to friends or colleagues in a fraction of a second, anywhere in the world. You can also attach files to your message e.g. a scanned photograph, a spreadsheet file etc. E-mail is fast, cheap and virtually free, because it takes so little time to download messages. You can compose e-mails off-line, and then send them all together, while you are receiving new e-mails at the same time. The following is an example of an e-mail message:

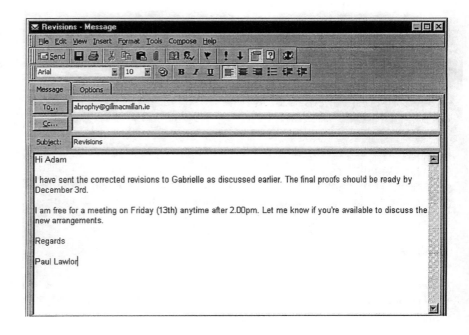

E-mail messages are also broken up into discrete parcels of data, which are then sent (or routed) around the world to their final destination. For example, an e-mail message could travel along the following paths in order to reach its destination:

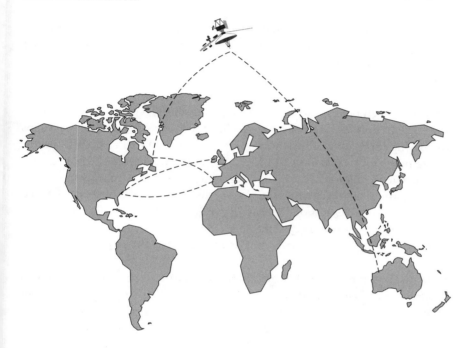

You can view a map of the Internet, as an e-mail message would see it, at www.peacockmaps.com. E-mail messages must be addressed in order to reach the person they are intended for. E-mails have a special address system, which has the following format:

- yourname@company.com
- yourname@company.ie

This is an example of an e-mail address: abrophy@gillmacmillan.ie

where:

- abrophy — Indicates the name of the person. You must place the name at the beginning of the address.
- @ — Indicates the (at) sign, which must follow the name.
- gillmacmillan — Indicates the company or organisation name, in this case Gill & Macmillan.
- ie — Indicates Ireland.

Some organisations offer free e-mail e.g. hotmail.com and ireland.com. In this case an e-mail address looks like the following:

joesoap@ireland.com

When you open an e-mail account with companies like these, you must visit their Web sites to send and retrieve your e-mail. You do not need to do this when you use the e-mail service provided by your ISP.

What Is USENET?

Another reason people surf the net is to join discussion groups or, as they are more commonly called, newsgroups. There are around 25,000 newsgroups discussing thousands of topics ranging from tropical fish to the VW Beetle. These newsgroups make up USENET. Normally you are required to register before you are allowed to join a newsgroup. Once you're registered you are free to join in the discussion. Of course, these discussions consist of typed messages, not talk, although that day is close at hand. (Don't confuse newsgroups where people type messages, with voice telephony where people talk with each other in the same way as you use a telephone.)

USENET was started in 1979 by American computer science graduates who thought that many people have a better chance of solving a problem than only one or two. Most of these problems centered on the UNIX operating system. Many newsgroups exist for the purpose of solving problems, but there are many that exist solely for the sake of a good argument.

The newsgroup name usually indicates what the newsgroup is discussing, but there is no way of knowing unless you join. For example, astron.sci is probably a newsgroup related to astronomy, but it might not be.

Newsgroups are useful if you have a particular problem and don't know where to find help. Just join a newsgroup dedicated to your topic, e.g. gardening, post a message and read the replies.

To read a newsgroup you need a newsreader! Microsoft's Outlook Express contains a newsreader (as well as e-mail). Some are free e.g. Free Agent, which you can download from the Internet at:

http://www.forteinc.com/getfa/getfa.htm

Many ISPs have newsreaders as part of their package. Once you download a list of newsgroups you see that they are organised into categories, for example: *biz* indicates commercial, *alt* indicates alternative, *comp* indicates computers and *sci* indicates science etc. Like e-mail, you can download headers (basic details of the discussion) and read them offline. This reduces your phone bill. Click on a header to see the replies (called the thread).

You can filter a particular group to remove messages from a particular person or subject you find annoying.

'USENET is like TETRIS for people who still know how to read.'
Computer Museum, Boston

Before you rush off to post a message, be aware of a few rules of thumb. Don't change the subject by posting a message on an on-going thread, start a new thread instead.

Netiquette

Don't 'spam' i.e. don't send junk e-mail messages or advertising to everyone in the group. Finally think before you post a message. Posting a message in a newsgroup is equivalent to publishing it, and therefore the same libel laws come into force. It is easy to get angry (flame) and post a bad-tempered message about somebody in a newsgroup (especially if they're new, a 'newbie'). This can be hurtful, but mostly this is simply embarrassing for the rest of the group. If you do post a message that you want to retract you can send a cancel message. However, if someone has already downloaded the thread, then it is too late. There are dedicated newsgroups for people who enjoy nothing more than a good argument e.g. alt.flame.

File transfer means the ability to move or transfer files from one computer to another. More commonly called FTP or File Transfer Protocol, it is used extensively when uploading a Web site or downloading files from the Internet. It allows you to transfer files or programs from one machine e.g. from your desktop to a Web server. So, what kind of software do you want to download? Well if you're like me, free stuff! Free software comes in different forms. Some of it is genuinely free and is called freeware, which means that it is yours and there are no restrictions on how you use it. Another type of free software is called shareware. This software is free only for a trial period. If you like it you are encouraged to buy it. Sometimes the shareware will have a function disabled e.g. the Save function, or it will cease to work after a defined period of time. Shareware relies on honesty, so if you try a program and like it, you should pay for it (normally the payment is small). Finally you can try beta versions of software. Beta versions are similar to a prototype of the final version.

What Is FTP?

Accessing
FTP SITES

'The Internet is so big, so powerful and pointless that for some people it is a complete substitute for life.'
Andrew Brown

FTP sites show what the Web looked like before the graphical user interface (GUI) was developed. GUIs make it easy to navigate today. When you first go into an FTP site you see the ROOT DIRECTORY with directory names. Some FTP sites restrict users to a PUB (public) directory where you find the downloadable files. Apart from the file name, you also see the date the file was uploaded, and its size. When you find a file you want, click on it and it usually downloads automatically. Always check files for viruses before you download. Finding a file from the list of FTP sites can be daunting, but there is a search engine called Archie available. However, you must know the exact name of the file you are looking for. The following sites have software, which you can download:

http://www.download.com
http://www.shareware.com
http://www.tucows.com

Using
CHAT-ROOMS

Chat-rooms are locations on the Internet where people can have a 'conversation' using typed messages, not talk. They are very popular, because they offer complete anonymity. You can't tell whether somebody is fourteen or eighty years old, male or female, from Seattle or Cavan. IRC (Internet Relay Chat) uses a chat server, which is linked with a network. These networks can host hundreds of channels, each devoted to a particular topic. There are organised events and special guests on some of these channels. Web sites also offer chat-rooms, which are easier to participate in, because you don't need special software.

Chatiquette

Remember that when you are in a chat room, you are typing a message that someone else is going to read. DON'T TYPE IN CAPITALS, because this is interpreted as shouting. Some people use symbols to indicate whether they're pleased or unhappy, for example, :-) 'smilies' and :('frownies'. They also use three letter acronyms (TLAs). Some examples of TLAs are: LOL – lots of love, OTOH – on the other hand etc. You can get a full listing at http://www.netlingo.com. TLAs can improve your speed when typing, but use them with discretion. Some people hate them! Never give any personal information in a chat-room e.g. a telephone number, your real name, credit card details or password etc. Use a name, which does not indicate your gender. Protect your identity at all times.

The Web

The Web is undoubtedly the part of the Internet that most of us are familiar with. The Web is a GUI (graphical user interface) and to surf it, all you have to do is to point and click. The Web contains millions of pages with text, pictures, sound and video. Most pages contain links to other pages. There is a wide diversity of sites ranging from banks, magic shows and homepages of 'Jeff on the beach' to libraries, stock exchanges and schools. Practically anything you can think of is on the Web. Some sites are worthless; some are extremely useful. Either way, the information is available and usually for free.

To surf the Web you need a browser. Most computers come equipped with a browser as standard. Browsers like Navigator (Netscape) and Internet Explorer (Microsoft) are the most common. When you launch the browser, you will be taken to a home page (either one you specified or the default page for the ISP). Then it's time to surf.

Using
BROWSERS

At the top of the page, you see an address box. This holds the Web address or URL (Uniform Resource Locator) of the site you want. The address is made up of different parts, for example, http://www.gillmacmillan.ie

'The Net is a waste of time, and that's exactly what's right about it.'
William Gibson

where:

- *http://* indicates the protocol, which is hypertext transfer protocol
- *www* indicates the site is hosted on a Web server (World Wide Web)
- *gillmacmillan* indicates the domain name
- *ie* indicates the name of the country, Ireland

If you know an address, you can simply type it in the address box. The Forward and Back buttons allow you to move between pages. If you visit a number of sites frequently you can bookmark them and make it easier to visit them in the future.

Your computer holds information about the sites you visit in a cache, which speeds up access. Some sites also add cookies, which are text files that show you what you did the last time you visited the site. If you don't like the idea of complete strangers saving information to your hard disk, turn off the cookie feature.

Cache &
COOKIES

Searching the Web for information will be one of the most common tasks you will be required to do. The information on the Web is not organised in any particular way. However, you can use search engines to search the Web and create a list of sites that match your requirements. Some of the search engines use automated programs that trawl the Web collecting information about each site that they visit. These engines are sometimes called bots, spiders or crawlers. Other engines are search directories that people have created based on the sites they have looked at. They then place the sites in a particular group e.g. education, health, or travel etc. These directories are split into smaller directories e.g. travel may be split into Europe, America and Africa etc. The following are some of the more common search engines:

• Yahoo — http://www.yahoo.com
• Lycos — http://www.lycos.com
• AltaVista — http://www.altavista.com
• Hotbot — http://www.hotbot.com
• Webcrawler — http://www.webcrawler.com

Since you already know about searching a database, using the search engines should not be a problem for you. If you type in a single word e.g. the word *free* you will get millions of hits, because the search engine lists any Web page with the word *free*. Entering *free + software* yields only pages that contain the words *free* and *software*. The plus sign (+) means that the word after it must be included. Using a minus sign (-) removes the word from the search list. So, *+free+software-shareware* lists sites with free software, but not including shareware. You can use wildcards in your searches. An asterisk (*) allows you to ignore text where the asterisk is placed. A question mark (?) allows you to ignore just one character. You can also use the following in your searches:

• Title: John's Homepage — Searches for pages with the title 'John's Homepage'
• Url: www.scoilnet.ie — Searches for the URL address of scoilnet.ie
• Anchor: — Searches for words contained in links
• Host:*ie — Searches for files in Ireland only

Building your own Web pages can be fun and remarkably easy to do. Of course, if you want to do it the hard way, you can use Hypertext Markup Language (HTML). HTML is not difficult to learn. However, many publishing packages are available, which can help you to create a Web page. It is more efficient and easier to use one of the publishing programs such as Microsoft Word, Microsoft Publisher, Front Page, Express or Composer to build your Web site. Most programs use wizards to guide you through the process.

Web-page design is important in presenting how your site looks and 'feels' to a visitor. Large graphics are not recommended. If you want to use a large graphic on a web page, at least use a thumb-nail graphic (small version) as a link to the larger one. In this way, the page loads faster and the visitor can choose whether to view the large graphic or not.

Too much text on a screen is another common mistake. Remember that you've got loads of space, so use it. Overloading a screen with text will not enhance your reputation as a Webmaster! Keep sentences clear and uncluttered. Insert hyperlinks to other pages, both within your own site, and to other relevant sites. Hyperlinks can be a mixture of text or icons. Include a link to your e-mail address. This is important for getting feedback from people who visit your site.

Don't use 'blinking text', which went out of fashion years ago. Use animated icons sparingly. You can use sound and video, but allow visitors to choose whether they want to listen to Beethoven's Fifth Symphony or view your favourite home video. If you're still unsure about what constitutes a bad Web page, browse the Web. Plenty of sites specialise in publishing poorly designed Web pages.

Once you've uploaded your Web page (ask your ISP how to do this) you want people to notice it. You can do this by telling the search engines you've arrived. Instead of going to each engine individually, you can submit to them all using http://www.submit-it.com. You can also add a counter that measures the number of 'hits' you receive.

Getting Noticed